Tomorrow

At

Eight

The Story of a Man, Who Has
Cerebral Palsy, And His Relationship
With One of His Care Providers.

By

Joe Leroy Hemphill

ISBN-13: 978-1490994703
ISBN-10: 149099470X

Tomorrow At Eight

Joe and Charity, his care provider.

Photo on facing page: Party time with Mable, Linda, and Joe.

Tomorrow At Eight

Living With Cerebral Palsy
And Working With Care Providers

By
Joe Leroy Hemphill

Edited By
Linda Sue Foster

Dedication

I have been living independently for the last forty years. I would not have been able to do this, without the help and encouragement of the many people who have been my care providers. There were times when they went way beyond the call of duty of care providers. I would not be so successful without these people. I dedicate this book to these wonderful individuals.

Linda, Joe, and Mable celebrating Joe's 70th Birthday.

Mable and Joe on a trip to Monterey.

Claudia and Joe

Other Books by Joe Leroy Hemphill

Keeping Up With Jerry, Published in 2010

It Has Been A Great Ride, Published in 2011

Approaching Seventy In The Bike Lane,

Published in 2014

All of Joe's books are available through
Amazon.com.

Joe enjoying the choice of chocolate milk, coffee, or water.

Table of Contents

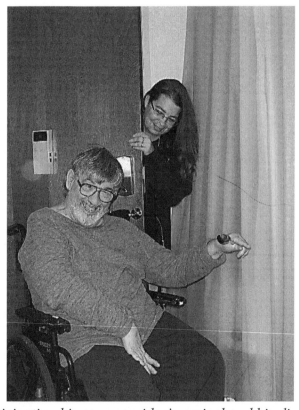

Anticipating his care provider's arrival and his dinner,
Joe is holding a spoon.

Preface

This book is a fictional account of my relationship with a care provider. In writing these pages, I hoped to share what it is like to need help with every aspect of your life. And how, many times, people who were my care providers became part of my life.

Two years ago, I went to the wedding of one of my providers. It was a special day for me, as she is a special person in my life. Another lady, who is one of my providers, has known me over twenty years and is the editor of this book.

It is not always easy being my care provider. I do have days when I am in a bad mood for one reason or another. Everyone has days like this. But, in my situation, I need to eat and have a shower, even though I feel bad. Unfortunately, my providers must give me the help I need, while putting up with my bad moods. In my defense, I must point out, my bad moods have decreased with age.

In my twenties, I lived in a residential care facility. Before I moved out of the care facility, there were not any programs that would allow someone like me to live in his own apartment. A social worker convinced her higher up to let five individuals, like me, live outside of a hospital setting.

The first two years were rough. My first care provider was good but he moved out of state to be with his girlfriend. My second provider had a drinking problem. Then I met a guy named Ed and he decided to become my roommate and care provider. We lived happily together for about two years. Then he got married. But, by the time Ed left, I was attending Long Beach State and found some good students who became my providers. Shortly after this, I began to get involved with an independent living center where I found more individuals to become providers.

After some years, finding providers, who were good, became harder and harder. So, when a friend offered to share her home with me, I took her up on the idea. She still is one of my providers. After about five years of living with her, I decided to go back to living by myself. I now live in a beautiful old building that was once a hospital. It was converted into apartments for individuals who are elderly and/or have disabilities.

Three years ago, after about a month stay in a hospital, we decided that I needed someone with me twenty-four hours a day. I realized I needed to make this change, but it was hard to let go of my independence and private time alone. I still am in charge of whom I have taking care of me. I will do this as long as I can.

In a section of this book, I mention some of the individuals, who wanted to be care providers, and who I did not describe in a favorable way. So, I want to say that most of the providers that I had were extremely good people and treated me with the utmost kindness and respect. While working for me, people become family. We have birthday parties and Christmas gatherings together.

Reading this book, I hope you will develop a sense of what it is to be a care provider and appreciate what they do for persons with disabilities. Incidentally, I am always taking applications.

Joe enjoying a strawberry ice cream sundae.

Joe working at his computer.

Joe playing Santa Claus.

Introduction
And Some Background on This Book

By Linda Foster - Long Time Friend, Care Provider, Proof Reader, and Book Editor.

Linda and Joe at Morro Bay

Joe was working on this book, when I first met him in 1992. He would crank out copies on a dot matrix printer. The copies were accordion pleated and were supposed to fold up in a box on the floor in front of his printer. Sometimes they did, and sometimes they didn't.

Also, after Joe moved into my house, my cat decided she liked to sleep in the box that held the blank paper for the printer. Her other favorite spot was on top of the template that fit over Joe's keyboard. This template had holes in it positioned over all the keys on his keyboard. This allowed Joe to poke a stick or stylus into the holes and push on them one key at a time. At least, when there wasn't a cat sleeping there.

I started helping with proofing right away. Joe had been working on this story for five years at that point. I realized the manuscript had some issues with tense, such as mixing past and past perfect tense. And, with the person it was written in, first person or third person or omnipresent narrator. I believe these things occurred because it took so long for Joe to write his stories. By the time he was working on a later chapter, he had forgotten the tense and narrator he had chosen for the beginning chapters.

I have to admit, back then I wasn't completely sure how some of these things worked. I honestly didn't know how to mix past tense and past perfect tense.

So, we hammered out how he wanted it to be, and looked up how to write it that way. Then I started changing it so it was consistent. I had to keep his voice, while making the grammar usage better, the spelling correct, the tense consistent, and the narrator in the third person, not the first.

We both learned a lot about correct English usage and

writing style. We had studied these issues in English classes in high school and college, but actually incorporating them into a manuscript was tricky.

Then, after many hours of work, Joe put this book on the shelf and kind of forgot about it for a number of years, while he was working on other projects. A friend of mine, and her mother, did some additional editing and printed a few copies for Joe, so he would have printed copies of his book. The copies went on the shelf.

Getting a book published back then was tricky and expensive. You usually just ended up with rejection slip after rejection slip. That is demoralizing and gets expensive with the printing and postage and such.

After moving to central California, we realized that just getting his writing out there for people to read was more important than trying to get a publisher to take an interest. With the help of his former short story writing teacher, Joe worked on writing essays. Essays worked well for letters and articles for the newspaper.

Joe had previously written letters to the editor and been published several times. Using his new essay writing skills, he started writing even more letters to the editor of the local newspaper. This worked quite well.

He also wrote articles for what the paper calls Valley Voices. He had a number of these letters and articles published. We have included many of them in two of his previous books, *It Has Been A Great Ride* and

Approaching Seventy In The Bike Lane, which are available on Amazon.com or directly from Joe. These are both collections of his writing, including short stories, articles, essays, letters, and poems.

Technology and the Internet eventually provided a way for us to publish his writing without the rejection slips, costs, and contracts. Amazon.com, which sells books through an online website, also developed and offered a free (major selling point) website where people could publish their own writing. This was exciting and a bit scary too. After all the rejection slips, it seemed too easy to simply publish his books himself without going through a publishing company.

We checked it out, read all the requirements, played around with it a bit, and realized we could do this. We kept the first book simple, with no photographs, and a stock photo for the cover that the site, CreateSpace.com, offered free. They do not charge for putting your manuscript into their system, either.

You have to do all your own typing, spell checking, formatting, proofing, editing, photo cropping, and meeting their specifications for printing. So, it takes a while to get it right. After you order and double check a proof copy or two, you are ready to go. Then, all you do is order and pay for the number of copies you want, plus the shipping. They print them, ship them to you, and you have published your book.

You can order one copy or a hundred or more. They charge per book, based on the number of pages, and give you better rates on larger orders. Smaller books, such as this are only a few dollars per book. At these prices, Joe can even give them as gifts to friends and family. You can sell them online on Amazon's site. You can also make your book available for other booksellers, libraries, and electronic media. In other words, everywhere. They assign you an ISBN number, so your book is official.

It is a fantastic idea and changed everything for Joe. He finally got his writing published and he loves every minute of it. We have published three books this way and this one will be the fourth. A fifth book is in the pipeline. It will be a book of prayers.

Upon learning that Joe has been such a prolific writer for over fifty years, people are usually amazed when they hear that Joe has never been able to read. He can read a little bit, but not actually enough to read a book in print or on his computer screen. And, in addition, he could never hold a book or turn the pages due to his cerebral palsy. Cerebral palsy quite often damages the nerves that control fine motor movements, as it did in Joe's case.

Knowing Joe, and being involved in his life for the past twenty-four years, has been quite an experience. I thought disabled people stayed at home, watched TV, and lived quiet lives. Ha! I sure was wrong about that; at least as far as Joe's life was concerned. His whole existence is an absolute whirlwind of activity and people coming and going.

In addition to the usual activity surrounding Joe, he has had several episodes of medical issues and hospitalizations over the past few years. These added greatly to the general feeling of not knowing what would happen next. While, at the same time, knowing that something would happen. I realized many years ago that my life is quiet and sedate, but his sure isn't.

The people, who work for him as care providers, make his life work and keep him out of institutions. Joe has lived in institutions and he knows he does not want to go back to that way of living.

It does get crazy, juggling care providers, their lives, and Joe's life around the clock, 24-7. But, in spite of it all, Joe still wouldn't trade the occasional insanity of his current situation for life in a nursing home or care facility for people with cerebral palsy.

Living independently, Joe can live his life the way he wants to, get up when he wants to, eat when he wants to, and most importantly, eat what he wants to. He can watch movies and the news on the Internet all night, if he wants to. He can listen to books on CD during breakfast and have friends over to celebrate birthdays and holidays.

He has a say in what happens in his life, who works for him, their schedules, and what they are expected to do on the job. He hires and fires his care providers and sometimes keeps them around for fifteen or twenty years. Most of these things would be impossible or not allowed in an institutional environment.

There have been many, many people in and out of Joe's life as care providers. Some were great, some were questionable, some told jokes, or were good cooks. There have been those who played chess or checkers with him, or expanded his life in various ways.

Some of his care providers have become like sons or daughters to Joe. He has also enjoyed their spouses, children, and siblings being involved in his life. He has gotten to be part of many special events in the lives of the people who work for him. He has enjoyed weddings, births, Christmas, First Communions, and been there to help them through the loss of their loved ones. Just as they have been there to help him through losses and setbacks.

Being a care provider for another person is, by circumstance and necessity, a very personal and intimate relationship. The situation and relationship can move in many directions and can even change over the years. Joe knows this all too well.

This book gives the reader an insight into the constantly surprising, sometimes scary, and always interesting twists, turns, ups, downs, sad, and happy events in the life of an incredible guy. His days consist of just trying to arrange for his next meal, keeping up with listening to books, and writing his stories.

He also stays busy emailing people, writing comments on Facebook, visiting with friends on the phone, on Skype, and in person, and not missing any of the juicy bits of life.

Remarks and Observations
By RaeLene Craver - Staff Supervisor

RaeLene and Joe at Joe's 70th Birthday Bash

I am the staff supervisor from an agency that helps "The Writer," Joe Hemphill, find care providers to work for him and keep him safe, healthy, and happy. I have been doing this for Joe for five years. I am involved with recruiting, pre-qualifying, and arranging interviews with candidates, who might be a good fit, for Joe to meet.

All the interviews, with so many different personalities, and working with the staff we eventually hire, certainly keeps things interesting. I feel like I continue to learn new things from all the people that have passed through Joe's life and all the situations that have come up.

Our experience of life is a roller coaster ride with all the ups-and-downs of what we go through. Try to imagine the experience through Joe's eyes. Then you will truly get a glimpse of his life. You will then know a different side of yourself, as well as a greater sense of respect for those who face much more challenging hurdles through life.

Caring, humor, intelligence, and sincerity are words that best describe "The Writer," Joe Hemphill.

By Mable Gilstrap - Chess Playing Friend, and Care Provider

Joe and Mable at Joe's 70th Birthday Party

Joe is one remarkable person. He is extremely physically handicapped from cerebral palsy. However, he has a very sharp mind. I have been one of his care providers for seventeen years. We, as care providers, make his life work. As his care provider, you have to do all of his daily care from feeding to bathing, as he cannot do these things for himself.

In the past, he took me to college with him to be his translator, because he has a speech problem. I learned a lot from doing this, as I sat in his writing class with him. I decided to write a cookbook featuring Joe's favorite recipes and meals. It explains how to fix his food in a way that keeps the food from choking him, as he has chewing and swallowing difficulties, but also keeps the texture and flavor pleasing to him.

When I am around Joe, we have fun. Linda, another friend and care provider, has taken the three of us on numerous trips to the mountains, including Yosemite, and over to the ocean. We have done day trips to many of the small towns here in the Central Valley and in the foothills of the Sierras. We have visited local museums, the zoo, the county fair, parks, wildlife preserves, and other nearby attractions.

We have had some good times doing these things. We have come to be close friends, the three of us. However, it is getting much harder to make these trips work out for us now. We are all getting older.

Joe fills your life with hope and makes you feel like trying to do anything that you want to do. He has encouraged me to improve my reading and writing abilities.

One day, Joe was writing a story about a gopher. I read the story and I liked it. He wanted to give up on it. But, I said don't; it will work! His first book to be published, *Keeping Up With Jerry*, was the result. So, I feel somewhat responsible for getting that book completed and published. It might never have happened, if I had not convinced Joe it would work. I remind him of that every chance I get.

Some Thoughts About Joe
By Areli - Joe's Care Provider

Joe, at first sight, might only seem like a man with a disability and a speech problem. What people do not see is that Joe is just like any one of us and probably a better person. Joe has a determination like no other. He has written three books with a stick that he pokes through holes in a template over his computer keyboard. By observing him do this, I can tell he has a will to be able to do anything, no matter how long it might take him.

He wants people to understand that a disability is just that, a disability. A disability is not who the person is. It might cause some limitations to that individual, but they have other qualities that make them unique.

Joe always says that people think that his life is the same every day. To their surprise, it is never the same;

every day is different. On any given day, he could have many calls to make, or interviews to do for new staff, or appointments, or issues to solve. No day is the same as another one for Joe.

He has a big heart. If, he sees someone having a tough day or who looks sad, he wants to go over and try to console the person. He is always trying to help families by informing them on disability issues through his letter writing to the Fresno Bee Newspaper, the articles he writes for the local UCP website, and the books he writes.

Even though Joe has a speech problem, he is a talker. Of course, sometimes people might not understand him. But, for those who want to take the time, he takes out his letter board and spells out what he wants to say. When he has someone with him, that is able to translate, he will talk and say what is on his mind. Joe tends to charm everyone he meets.

Working For Joe
By Mary Arens - Care Provider

It has been four years since I first met Joe and started working for him. I had been working for one of his neighbors for many years before that. So, we had seen each other and said hi many times.

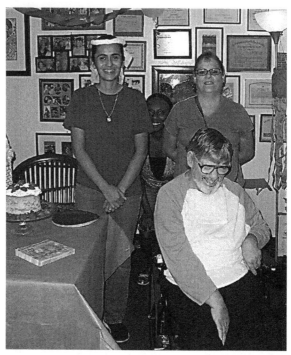

Party time at Joe's apartment. Areli, Josie, Mary, and Joe.

A friend was working for Joe at the time and she knew he was looking for someone to work for him. She brought me over to Joe's to introduce me to him. Joe and I hit it off and he asked me if I wanted to start right away and have my friend train me. I said yes and that was the beginning of my experience working for Joe.

When Joe found out I could cook, he was excited. One of his favorite things for me to cook is chicken fried cube steak with gravy and mashed potatoes. I also fix hamburgers, the way he loves them, with bar-be-que sauce, pickle relish, cheese, mayo, ketchup, lettuce, onions and made with the bread he likes instead of a bun. He also likes it when I fix ground beef tacos with no tortillas and just the filling on the plate. When I work in the morning, I fix him an omelet with lots of veggies and cheese, just the way he likes it.

About six months ago, I was in a serious car accident. Joe and several of his other care providers came by to see me in the hospital. I couldn't work for six months. I just recently was released to come back to work part time. I am happy to be back to work and I made a hamburger for Joe's dinner on my first real day back.

Joe was patient with me, while I was out. He encouraged me to get better and strong enough to return to work. A typical man, I am sure all he really missed was my cooking.

I am very grateful to Joe for keeping a spot open for me to come back and work for him. Working for Joe is like being with family and we all take care of each other.

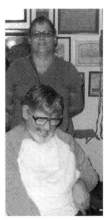

Joe and Mary

Meeting Joe Hemphill
By Charity Rogers Monge - Care Provider

Charity and Joe

I met Joe when I first applied to work for an agency as a care provider. I was scheduled to have an interview at the apartment building where Joe lives. When I first walked into Joe's apartment, I'll admit my stomach was filled with butterflies. I didn't know if this man was going to like me or if he was going to throw me out. I was not quite sure what to expect. I had never applied nor worked in this field before.

A presentable, very much younger, blonde woman came out to what I thought was the waiting room and called my name, Charity Rogers. I thought to myself, "Ok, Charity, this is it! Put your best foot forward and be yourself. If it works, and it's Gods will, then Joe will love you."

The woman that had called my name, told me she was the supervisor, and then she explained about Joe's speech difficulty. "When Joe is talking to you, you won't be able to understand, so he has an interpreter here to tell you what he is saying."

My first thought was, oh great he doesn't speak English!!

She continued, "But please look at him when he is speaking, at all costs, because he becomes offended, if you do not, and speak directly to him when you reply."

When I walked in, my first impression was completely different from the picture I had painted in my head. This man sitting in front of me was in a wheelchair, with glasses. He was so cute with his salt and pepper hair. So, then I walked right up and said, "Hi, my name is Charity Rogers and I'm very pleased to meet you Joe….um I'm not sure of your last name yet."

Then he spoke and I couldn't understand because he has a speech disorder. Then I understood what the supervisor was talking about. Joe had a care provider there to tell me everything he expected from me, if I got the job.

Then the interview was over and I went home. About an hour later, I received a call from the supervisor asking me if I was truly serious about coming to work for her and Joe. Without any hesitation, I answered her, "Yes." I truly felt comfortable when I was in the interview. I had already fallen in love with the supervisor, Joe, and the care provider. It all just seemed a natural fit for me.

There are so many people in the world today with able bodies, legs that can walk, and mouths that can speak. But, Joe wasn't born with those privileges and he has never let that hold him back. Since I have worked for this man, I have learned about all the therapies he had to undergo and challenges he had to face, but he still pushes on.

I see and meet people every day who complain about their lives. They say they are not able to (or cannot or will not) do anything to better themselves. I tell them that I have a friend, who has cerebral palsy, and who endures dealing with a speech problem every day of his life. And, he graduated from high school, went to college, and now has published three books and is working on his fourth book as we speak. He has not had anything handed to him. I admire Joe for the struggles he has gone through and his perseverance to overcome it all, despite what life has given him. And, he has taught me a great deal about being a care provider.

Over the three years that I have worked for Joe, I have come and gone a few times. I have learned a lot from the past few times that Joe has fired me. But, I must say, the last time Joe let me go was the hardest. At first, I couldn't understand why he let me go. But, since I've been gone for this past year, I have come to the conclusion and realization that it is frustrating to him when I still don't understand what he is saying. I also needed to take a step back and realize that I can't bring my personal life to work. My personal life and work need to be separated, even though Joe is the easiest person to talk to.

I came back to work for Joe to be able to show him that I have grown as an employee. I have learned to never get too comfortable, because this is a place of business not my home. Joe has taught me that. Also, to show him that no matter what differences we had in the past, when he needs me, I will always be there for him. And, I've learned that Joe is and always will be my boss and that's how he will be treated, with respect.

I love to see Joe happy, content, and healthy. And, involved in his writing, because boy does he love to write and he can do it too! He deserves that.

I'd like to see all his friends, family, and care providers, old and new, get together with him and have a party. And just celebrate Joe Hemphill because Joe isn't told enough how much he is appreciated. And, he should be, despite the fact that he is the one cared for, as he does a lot of caring for other people.

I am glad to have had the pleasure of meeting and taking care of Joe and continuing the care of him. He forever will be the man that opened the doors to a new and exciting world for me and I thank him for that. If you ever get a chance to pop by and meet Joe, you might find something your life has been missing.

My New Boss, Joe
By Claudia Young – Care Provider

When I first walked through Joe's door, I knew I was in for a challenge. But, as my instructor was training me, I kind of knew it wouldn't be that hard.

Joe is very hard to understand, as everyone had explained to me. I knew a few words he was trying to say to me. I read the book that Joe had written about his life. He had given it to me so I would understand a little more about his background. I read it while training to be hired on permanently. As a month passed and I started to work by myself, I became more aware of how Joe's program worked for the night shift.

I have been here almost five months and I absolutely enjoy every time I see Joe. The best parts of my nights here are when Joe smiles after he hears me saying something funny. His smile is priceless.

I enjoy working for Joe and would not change it for anything in the world.

Claudia and Joe

Biography of Joe Leroy Hemphill

Joe Hemphill has had cerebral palsy from birth. He has been a life-long learner and has dedicated much of his life to bettering the lives of other disabled people.

His writing focuses on informing the general public on issues involving people who have disabilities. He does this with humor and sensitivity by sharing details of his life, his struggles, and daily living challenges.

Joe is involved with life, his surroundings, and the people who are part of his life. He embraces life and gives hope to others.

About the Author
Joe Leroy Hemphill

Joe has been involved with many agencies and groups over the years. He has volunteered to help others and helped to raise money. He has donated his writing to non-profit groups and written numerous letters to the editor and opinion pieces for the local newspapers. And, he has been involved in his local community and nationally, making life better for everyone. A few of the things he has done.

<u>United Cerebral Palsy (UCP)</u>

In 1953, Joe was part of the UCP of Los Angeles telethon. He was ten years old and excited to be on stage with celebrities and to help raise money for UCP.

Joe has been involved with United Cerebral Palsy of Central California for about seventeen years. He started out by volunteering to help with their Quest Lab where different technologies were demonstrated. When Joe first started helping, UCP held the lab weekly for anyone who wanted to drop in. Parents, teachers, speech therapists, college teachers with their students, and care providers would come in alone or with very young children, older children, and adults with various disabilities.

The lab had a variety of computer programs, input devices, speech devices, joysticks, keyboards, etc., that people could try. This way, they could find out if a certain program or device would work, before buying it. Joe actually tried out speech devices there too and eventually found the Message Mate that he still uses.

Joe demonstrated his letter board, his speech device, and his computer keyboard with the acrylic template over it. He spoke to the families of young children. Families who were just beginning to search for technology that might help their child connect to the world. He demonstrated equipment and spoke to college teachers and their students, who were studying to be special education teachers or speech pathologists. One of his care providers, who understood his speech, usually had to be there too to help translate Joe's speech.

Joe appeared live on UCP of Central California telethons to help raise money. He also has done interviews on TV to help promote UCP.

Joe served on the Board of Directors for UCP of Central California for a few years. That was a great experience for him. He met many wonderful and caring people. He got involved with some of the aspects of the non-profit world.

He has written articles for the UCP of Central California web site to introduce UCP staff and board members. He has had many of his stories and articles published on their website. He has written letters to the editor of the local newspaper to bring attention to fundraising events for UCP.

Joe's articles also were published on the National UCP

organization's web site. He feels that he is paying UCP back for the help they have given him and others over the years.

Fresno City College - The Ram's Tale

Joe enrolled in fiction writing classes as many times as the college would allow. Then he did an independent study class with one of the English instructors at the college. Joe is still in touch with one of his former teachers there and receives input from him on current projects Joe is working on.

While a student at Fresno City College, Joe had two pieces of his writing selected for inclusion in The Ram's Tale, a collection of student art and literary work. His story, "A Jar of Jelly," was published in the 2002 edition. His non-fiction essay, "Even From a Wheelchair," was published in the 2006 edition. He won Second Prize Non-Fiction for that piece. Joe was very proud and excited to attend the awards ceremonies at the college.

National Public Radio (NPR) - Valley Public Radio - Valley Writers Read

On the advice of a friend, Joe also submitted some of his stories to Valley Public Radio for possible inclusion in their series, Valley Writers Read. His piece was selected to be part of the program. He had a friend read his piece and it sounded great over the radio. After the show aired on the radio, they sent a CD to Joe with his story on it. Then he had another piece accepted for being read on the air the following year. It was exciting and he may do it again in the near future.

Articles and Letters To The Editor

Joe has written many articles and letters to the editor. They have covered disability issues, the finding of, training, and keeping good care providers, and making sure care providers are paid fairly. Joe has also written about politics, legislation, laws, and many other issues that he feels strongly about.

California State University, Fresno

Teachers have invited Joe at least four times to Cal State, Fresno, to do presentations. He has demonstrated his speech device, letter board, shared his writing and books, and given speeches, via his care provider doing the talking and reading Joe's prepared text.

These presentations have gone well and they have asked him back. They have also referred him to other teachers there to do presentations for their classes. These events have been fun and quite gratifying for Joe and his care providers. He likes the idea of speaking directly to the next generation of special education teachers and speech pathologists.

Joe has a unique voice in the area of disabilities. These

speaking engagements before college students, who will soon be working as professionals in schools and other institutions, are wonderful. He has had the opportunity to open their minds to the creativity and intelligence of at least one disabled individual, who has not let anything get in his way or quiet his voice. He hopes to do more of these.

Joe (in the patterned vest) in the front row of a classroom full of students. His two care providers are standing behind him and to the right. You can see the cover of his book, "It Has Been A Great Ride," projected on the screen behind them to the left.

Tomorrow At Eight

By

Joe Leroy Hemphill

An old friend returns.
Old fears resurface.
Reunions are good.

Chapter 1

It was almost eight a.m. and Jerry was in bed waiting for Megan, his care provider, to show up to help him get out of bed. Five minutes passed and he wondered if Megan was going to be late. He knew she would be there as soon as her class was over. He never could understand how someone could take a math class at seven in the morning. His mind did not function until noon.

He had let his last aide go because she was three hours late, two days in a row. Some people who took the job of helping him didn't realize, if they didn't show up, he couldn't get dressed or eat. And, he liked to eat. Some people took this job because they thought it was a kick-back job, but it had a lot of responsibilities. If, he didn't get his medication at a reasonable time, his muscles would tighten up, and he wouldn't be able to do anything.

Megan had not helped him for over two years, while she had been away at college. It would be nice to see her again. He had known Megan since she was sixteen. She had lied about her age because he couldn't hire anyone under eighteen, but she had been one of his best helpers.

He preferred to call people, who assisted him, helpers or friends rather than aides.

A friend had fixed three switches by his bed. One to turn a light on and off, one that controlled his TV, and the third to turn his radio on and off. He hit the switch for the radio and country music filled his bedroom.

His apartment had two bedrooms and he used one of them as an office. All the light switches in the apartment had been lowered so he could reach them. And the bathroom door had been widened so his wheelchair could fit through it. A bar had been fixed to the floor so he could help himself on and off the toilet. The carpet was the commercial type with no padding, which made it easier to roll his wheelchair by pushing with his feet.

He didn't have enough control in his arms and hands to push his wheelchair using the rails attached to the wheels, as some people could do. There were bars in the shower for him to use but he still needed help. The landlord offered to lower the stove and the kitchen sink. There wasn't any need, since he couldn't cook for himself.

He looked at the clock again. Fifteen minutes had passed. If Megan had forgotten, he would have to start calling his backup aides. Sometimes, Sandy didn't have to go into work at the clothing store until noon. Gary, another backup aide, works a night job, and arrives home about nine. What a way to start the day!

He kicked the covers off. It was chilly in the morning in March. He reminded himself that this was better than living in a hospital. He had left his pajama bottoms half down in case he needed to climb out of bed in the middle of the night and make his way into the bathroom.

He swung his legs off the edge of the bed, pulled himself up on his elbow into a sitting position, as they had taught him in day school when he was young. He hadn't had so much weight to pull up then. People with cerebral palsy usually don't gain much weight because they burn up so much energy from involuntary movements. Getting out of bed this way burned a lot of energy.

He next made sure that he had locked the brakes on his wheelchair. Then he grabbed hold of the makeshift grab bar screwed into the bookcase. The bookcase was merely some two-by-fours and some paneling nailed together. As he pulled himself up and started to swing himself into his chair, the whole bookcase started to move.

Just then, Megan walked in. "Jerry!" She rushed over and guided him into his chair. "What were you doing? I told you that I would be here."

He told her, "A little excitement in the morning is good to get my heart going." He made light of the situation to keep her from becoming upset. He looked up and noticed her brown hair was fuller than the last time he had seen her. There was a mole on her upper lip. She was wearing overalls with a T-shirt under them.

"I thought Jack, your past helper, was going to fix that bookcase so that it wouldn't move when you grabbed the bar."

He replied, "Jack wasn't worth the money for the paper his last check was written on."

"Sorry to hear that." She wheeled Jerry into the bathroom and he took hold of the bar fixed next to the toilet helping himself onto the throne. "Be careful. You gave me enough excitement for my first day."

"I had to do something to welcome you back," Jerry said.

"Please, don't be so happy to see me." Megan started making the bed. "I was a little late because I stopped at the church to check on my new job."

"You are working at a church?" He laughed. "The girl who plays pool in bars until two in the morning?"

"Jerry, that was a long time ago and you're about the only one who knew me back then. Speaking of bars, I know a few things about you, remember? Getting pulled over in a wheelchair for drunk driving."

"We have both changed." A few seconds later. "I am ready," he called from the bathroom.

She helped him back into his chair, took off his pajamas, and wheeled him across to the railing next to the shower. He took hold of the railing, as she placed her hand around his waist. Then she held him steady as he stepped over the lip on the bottom of the shower. He had had the shower door removed, so it would be easier to get him in and out. She guided him into the shower chair, which was really made for someone who couldn't sit on the toilet, but it served him better in the shower. She pulled the shower curtain closed. Then she reached in one side of the curtain pointing the nozzle toward the wall away from him, in case the water came out too hot. He put his right arm under the water to test it.

Jerry said that the water was all right and she turned the nozzle to where his whole body could get wet. In a few seconds, she reached through the curtain, turned the nozzle away from him, and turned off the water. She opened the curtain and started to wash his back and chest.

"Do I get any toys to play with?"

"Maybe next time, if you're good. Pick up your legs." Her hands moved gently over his body until she had him all soaped. She shampooed his hair and then she closed the curtain turning the water back on so he could rinse off. She made the water warmer this time, so his muscles could relax for a few minutes, and left him there.

In a while, he called for her and she reached through the curtain and turned off the water. She opened the curtain and reached for a towel. "Feel better?"

"I de . . ."

"What?"

"Declare." He repeated.

"Declare."

"Yes. Declare."

"You and your fifty-cent words." She said, shaking her head.

"Anyway. I declare that I haven't had a good shower since the last time you took care of me."

She dried him and reached for the baby oil. She rubbed it all over him to keep his skin from itching. "I bet you say that to everybody who helps you."

"But I really mean it when I say it to you."

She then put some ointment on him, so he wouldn't get a rash from sitting all day in his wheelchair. He grabbed hold of the bar while she placed a towel long ways in his chair, and he stepped out of the shower and sat down. She wheeled him over to the sink where she shaved him and brushed his teeth. Then, she reached over to his clothes, which were on a towel rack in the bathroom. He placed his clothes there every night so whoever helped him would know what he wanted to wear. He had even picked out his clothes in the hospital, mainly to keep a little control over his own life.

Megan first slipped on his underwear over his feet and legs. Then, he pulled himself up by the bar next to the shower and she pulled his pants the rest of the way up. He reminded her to take the towel out of the wheelchair seat before he sat back down again. She picked up his shirt, putting his right arm in the sleeve first, because it was harder to bend than his left. After putting the left sleeve on, she then buttoned his shirt.

She bent down and put on his socks and shoes. She rubbed some styling gel in his hair and combed it. "Well, you look presentable. Are you ready for breakfast?"

"I am starved." He said.

She wheeled him out of the bedroom, down the hall, and into the dining room. He pulled himself up to the dining room table that Gary, one of his past helpers, had given him before moving out of state. Gary was one of the best helpers Jerry had hired in a while and he almost cried when Gary left.

Some people told him that he shouldn't become emotionally involved with the people who worked for him. It was hard not to when he saw them almost every day and they helped him with such personal things as cleaning him after he used the toilet.

Megan walked over to the stove. "What will it be today? And, remember, I have been away. Don't get fancy on my first day back."

He said, "Two eggs and some toast would be fine." He then asked, "Made up your mind on graduate school yet?"

She opened the refrigerator and retrieved two eggs and a loaf of bread. "Yes, I don't know if I told you, but I am hoping to be accepted by a college sometime in June." She started cooking. "Anyway, what is the name of the center where you work and what do you do there?"

"It is the Delgado Independent Living Center and I work two days a week." He said, speaking slowly so she could follow what he was saying. "I interpret new laws that relate to the disabled and I write articles for the newsletter."

"That sounds interesting." She finished cooking the eggs and toast, then brought them across to the table. She placed the toast in a dish and poured some milk over it so he could swallow it easier.

"You're right, but, each time that a chance at a promotion comes up, I am passed over and it's becoming a real drag. A friend told me that it was because of my speech defect, but my supervisor tells me that I don't have enough experience."

"That seems wrong." She put the spoon into his mouth and scraped the food off with his front teeth, since he couldn't close his mouth around the spoon.

After swallowing, he agreed. "I suspect the only reason why I was hired was to make The Center look good and to cover up the fact that the head of The Center was dating the guy who was supposed to be training me to take over publishing their newsletter."

"Jerry, relax. If you get too angry, you'll start coughing and won't be able to eat this great breakfast. Can't you rcport it to someone?"

"If I say anything, it might cause problems for the person who told me and she has been a good friend. She has been about the only one who has treated me half way nice."

"Still, it doesn't seem right."

He finished his eggs. "I just have six more weeks there and, if I am not promoted, I can get my old job back at Long Beach State College. The pay is lower but people respected me there."

"When would you start at Long Beach?"

"In two months."

"What did you do there?"

"Taught sex education."

"What?" She looked up in amazement.

"Got you!" He said laughing.

"Oh, yes, I forgot about your demented sense of humor."

"Seriously," he said, "I was the editor of the handicapped newsletter."

She gave him a bite of toast. "That sounds like an important job."

"It was just a title. I wrote most of the articles myself. But, I felt I was doing something useful, even though the pay wasn't much."

"Speaking of pay . . ."

"What, you want to be paid, in addition to getting to look at this body?"

"Jerry, your body wouldn't pay my rent, even if you were a body builder."

"Well, in that case the forms you need to sign are in my office. The forms say I pay four twenty-five per hour but I will pay you five dollars."

"Thanks, I could use it, but what do I have to do to earn it?"

Grinning, he replied. "I will think of something." He usually paid his helpers more than the state allowed. He had to supplement the pay to make it worth somebody's time to drive over.

"I don't paint walls or put in water lines." She poured some more milk on his toast to make the crusts soft.

He replied. "Then that shot my idea for tomorrow down the tubes." He took the bite of toast she offered him. "Do you realize I have known you since you were in high school?"

"Yes, and when I earn my doctoral degree, it will cost you three times as much to get me over here to wash your back." She cleaned his mouth where milk had run down his chin.

He protested. "I should get a discount for putting up with your crazy school schedule. Remember when I had to get up at six in the morning because you had a seven o'clock class?"

"It was good for you. It built character to get up early, old man."

"Maybe so, but I was working on my psychology homework all night in those days."

"Hey, if you want a good aide, you have to take me when I can get here."

"You didn't know anything about being an aide, before you met me."

"I made all my mistakes on you so I looked real good when I worked for someone else or in a rest home. You don't have any more bread. But, being such a good aide, I brought you some of my homemade cookies." She started to break the cookies up in the milk.

"Thanks for the cookies. By the way, who was the guy who answered the phone?"

"Oh, Rick. He is just a guy I met."

"You don't move in with 'just a guy'!"

"Well, I sort of like him a lot."

"Where did you meet?" Jerry asked.

"At one of the drug rehab hospitals."

"Are you doing all right?" He asked, looking closely at her.

"Oh, yes. That stuff is in the past."

"Does your mom still get on your case?"

"Every now and then but I can handle it. I am sure glad I had you to talk with in those days."

"That still goes." Jerry told her reassuringly.

"I know. I haven't told Rick about Mom," she explained.

"Some things are best left unsaid. You like him a lot?" Jerry grinned.

"Yes." She smiled and there was a glow about her face.

"Megan, I am happy for you."

"Thanks." She finished feeding him and then wheeled him back to the bathroom to wash the food out of his beard. After she had done that, she asked "Don't you need to get in your power wheelchair?"

"Yes. The bus will be here at ten."

"Then, I had better hustle my bustle. Need anything from your office?"

"My reading glasses and those folders on the right side of my computer."

She brushed his hair once more, pushed him into the hall, ran into the computer room, and grabbed his glasses and folders. She then pushed him the rest of the way into the living room over to where there was a grab bar fixed to the wall next to his electric wheelchair.

She locked the brakes on his manual wheelchair. He took hold of the bar, pulled himself up on his feet, swung across to his electric chair, and sat down. She flopped down the footrests and he put his feet on them so he could push himself back in the seat. Then she reached down beside him, found his seat belt, and fastened it.

She straightened his sweater and made sure he could reach the cloth he used to wipe his mouth when he drooled. She gave him a hug. "Have a good day." She opened the front door and they both went out.

The bus was waiting. Jerry drove his chair out the gate and she followed. The driver made a joke about not taking him "to the beach to watch girls," because, if he had to work, Jerry had to go to work too.

Jerry backed his wheelchair onto the lift, and it raised him and his chair up into the bus. While the driver was strapping Jerry's chair down, Jerry watched Megan cross the street and go into one of the buildings at the church.

The driver said, "That was a fine girl who came out with you." Jerry nodded. He sure was right.

You are late!

A trip through the neighborhood.
Jerry's friend, Craig.
Two tacos to go.

Chapter 2

In Jerry's apartment, the fluorescent light hovered above his computer as he slid the wooden dowel across the plastic template set half an inch above the keyboard. The template had holes positioned over each key. He aimed the dowel into the desired hole before pushing it into the hole and striking the key underneath. He moved the dowel quickly from hole to hole as letters and then words appeared on the blue screen.

He was working on a rough draft of an article detailing plans for building sixteen apartments designed for persons confined to wheelchairs. As he chose each word, he pondered whether this article would go into the handicapped newsletter. Or, would they just file it away like most of the work he wrote for The Center. He sat back and read the screen, activated the save command, and turned off his computer.

As the screen turned black, he rolled across to his right where a brown-topped table had the latest TV guide. He glanced at the list of programs. He then worked his left thumb under the blue cloth strap that held his reading glasses on and pulled it and the glasses up and over his head.

He then reached across the counter top to touch one of the three brown switches built into the counter. He accidentally hit the wrong switch, causing the overhead fan to start swirling around. He swiftly turned off the fan. Then he hit the correct switch to turn off the light.

Pushing his chair backward with both feet, he moved toward the door of his computer room and propelled himself down the hall into his living room. Crossing over to the coffee table, he retrieved his sunglasses, which had a black band that was once part of Megan's swimming suit. He slipped them on over his head, adjusting them on his face with both forearms.

He moved his manual wheelchair, which he mainly used indoors, across to where his electric wheelchair sat. Then he reached down and pulled out the black cord connected to the electric chair's charger.

The wheelchair was specially equipped with four lights, three in back, and one in front, for night driving. A friend had installed two car horns, which could be operated by stepping on a button. He wheeled his manual chair around to the front of his electric chair and set the locks on the manual one.

He grabbed hold of the bar fixed on the wall. He pulled himself up, swung his body across to his electric chair, and leaned against the edge of the seat. As he was sitting there, he used his right foot to flip down the footrest. Then, placing both feet on the one footrest, he pushed himself back into his electric chair. After getting his left foot on the other footrest, he then brought the seat belt across his torso and attached both pieces with Velcro.

He grasped the joystick, which made the electric chair move in whatever direction he pushed the handle of the joystick. He moved the handle a little toward the front door and then back toward the wall to test his chair and his arm control.

He checked the bag on the left side of his chair, to make sure he had his letter board. He used the letter board to spell words out for people who couldn't understand him. He also checked for the door key, that someone had attached to a pipe, so he could hold it to open his front door when he returned.

Everything seemed to be set so he put his hand on the joystick. Pushing it forward slowly, he moved his power chair into the middle of the living room, turned it around, and headed to the front door. When he reached the door, he needed to move the chair backward because the left footrest was blocking the door. So, moving the joystick towards himself, he backed up his electric wheelchair, which allowed him to clutch the knob, turn it, and open the door.

He locked the door from the inside. Then he let the door hit the padding nailed to the wall exactly where the doorknob would bang. He had the padding placed there after he had broken a mirror in the next-door apartment when he had come in too quickly and slammed his front door against the wall.

He moved the joystick forward and to his left. He drove his chair out the door and down the wooden ramp. Next, he turned his chair around and drove back up the ramp. He fished for the yellow cord, tied to the outside doorknob, and wrapped the cord around his right hand. With his left hand, he pulled back on the joystick backing up his chair and closing the door at the same time.

He then turned his chair around and started driving down the sidewalk. At the end of the sidewalk was Craig. Craig had red hair and was four years old. He was wearing a blue checked western shirt, rust colored pants, and cowboy boots that were too large for his feet.

Craig's mom had been Jerry's aide since soon after Craig was born and Jerry saw him almost every day. While still in diapers, Craig would sit on Jerry's kitchen table and attempt to feed him breakfast, getting half in Jerry's mouth and half on the table. Soon, Craig had discovered it was more enjoyable, and productive, to put one bite into Jerry's mouth and another into his own.

Today, Craig was vigorously rearranging the flowers along the sidewalk to make room for the underground garage he was digging for his miniature toy cars. The manager would have written up Craig's mother, if the manager had caught Craig playing in the flowers. Jerry didn't think it was fair that the housing project didn't have any playgrounds for children.

Jerry's brother, Lance, and he had enjoyed a whole

backyard to play in when they were growing up. And, in the summertime, most of their days from morning to nightfall were spent there.

In one corner, they had built a hideout with some old bricks and wood. Their Dad had brought the materials home from a storage shack on his last construction site.

In another corner were two wire hutches. One had Sue, Lance's rabbit, and in the other hutch was Jerry's rabbit, Roy.

Jerry's mom would put Jerry in a bamboo rocking chair just outside the back door. Then he would rock back and forth until he reached the hideout or the wire hutch holding Roy.

Every other day, Jerry would drag the water hose with him to water the apricot tree. For doing this, he earned twenty-five cents a week.

Each month or so Mom would take Jerry to the music store. The lady there would say the names of the most popular songs and he would indicate which one he wanted by making a sound. Mom always reminded Jerry not to be so loud when they weren't at home, but sometimes he would forget.

Jerry yelled, "No, Craig!" Craig pretended not to hear him and continued stirring up the dirt. Jerry drove his chair over to Craig and said, "Stop that, right now." Craig went right on digging. "Want some candy?" Jerry asked.

Craig immediately stopped his activity and his freckled face peered up with expectation. Jerry didn't think Craig was becoming hard of hearing or that he didn't understand him. They went too far back for that. Craig was merely developing a stubborn streak.

Craig searched the bag on Jerry's chair, which sometimes had candy. And, when Craig's investigation came up empty, he looked at Jerry with sad eyes. "What happened?"

"All gone."

"Can we go to the store?"

"Maybe. Help me get my mail." Jerry pointed to the key ring dangling on the side of his chair.

Craig climbed up on Jerry's lap, twisted around, and held onto both sides of his chair. "We go to the store?"

Jerry took the joystick and turned his chair left on the sidewalk toward the mailboxes. "Maybe later."

"Go fast?" Craig asked as his mom waved at them.

"Okay." Jerry moved the joystick forward, his chair sped down the sidewalk, making left turns, and then right turns. Soon the mailboxes were in sight and Craig started reaching down on the left side of the chair for the keys. Craig was about to fall out of Jerry's lap, trying to unhook them.

Jerry quickly let go of the joystick and the chair came to a swift stop. He grabbed Craig with both arms and yanked him back onto his lap. "Craig, hold on. Both hands."

"Why?"

"You'll fall and get hurt."

"Go to the store?"

"No." Jerry raised his voice. "Hold on."

"Are you mad?" Craig softly asked.

He held Craig close. "No, not mad. I just don't want you to get hurt."

"You hit me now?"

"Craig, I'd never hit you," Jerry explained.

"Grandma hit." Craig whispered.

He pulled Craig closer. "We're friends. We don't hit."

Craig turned and flung his tiny arms around Jerry's neck. Then Craig turned back around and held onto the sides of the chair and Jerry pushed the joystick forward and continued to the mail boxes.

Reaching the mail boxes, Jerry brought the joystick back to the center and the chair came to a stop. Craig peered up at him for permission. Jerry nodded and Craig climbed down from his lap and darted around to where the keys were dangling on the side of the chair. Craig held up two keys and Jerry pointed to the one for the mail box.

Craig tried three times before getting the key into the hole. Finally, he succeeded in putting the key into the lock and turned it. When Craig opened the box, all kinds of flyers, advertisements, and letters fell out onto the cement.

Craig bent his small wiry body down and commenced gathering up the pieces of mail. He held each piece up so Jerry could see it. If Jerry shook his head, Craig stuffed the flyer or advertisement into the black trash receptacle. If Jerry nodded, Craig jammed the letter into the pouch on the side of the wheelchair.

After all the mail was distributed, Craig climbed back onto Jerry's lap and held on with both hands. "Go to the store?"

"Not now." Jerry took the joystick and proceeded back to where Craig was constructing his underground garage.

Reaching the construction site, Craig once again climbed down off Jerry's lap. "Can we go to store later?"

"Yes, later." Craig's mom waved and nodded at Jerry. "You promise?"

Jerry nodded. As he pulled away, Craig began busying himself once again with his cars. Jerry guided his chair down the sidewalk, between two apartment buildings, and out into the alley that had carports on both sides.

People kept parking in Jerry's carport leaving his aides and friends with nowhere to park. He felt like having their cars towed away. But that would have started more hassles than he wanted.

Using the joystick, he guided his chair around and between the speed bumps. At the end of the alley, his chair rolled over the pressure plate in the driveway. This caused the electric gate to open and he drove his chair out onto the sidewalk.

At the corner of Hunt and Morgan Streets there were

signal lights going both ways. It was too much trouble trying to push the walk button. So, he eased his chair down a driveway toward the edge of the road.

When the light turned green and the cars making turns had passed through the intersection, he pushed the joystick all the way forward and sped across Hunt Street. He executed the same maneuver to cross Morgan Street.

Once, the psychologist at The Center saw Jerry crossing the street and became really upset and worried and wanted to talk to him about it. People said that this psychologist was an expert with helping disabled people work out their problems. From what Jerry had seen, the only thing the psychologist did was to have people wear rubber bands around their wrists and snap them every time they had a naughty thought. Jerry was certain that his not having enough control to snap the rubber band made him a poor patient.

Jerry traveled west along the sidewalk. He kept the joystick slightly toward the right, away from the traffic. He did this in the event his left arm or hand had an involuntary movement. This way, he and his chair would have less chance of flying off the sidewalk into oncoming cars. As a result of this tendency, he had ended up in the shrubbery bordering the sidewalk more than once.

Toward the end of the block, he turned his chair into the Jack-in-the-Box driveway on his right. There was a ramp, beside the driveway leading to the drive-thru window. When his chair reached the top of the ramp, a tall slender woman with blond hair took notice of him through the window.

Jerry had seen Peg at a few of the AA meetings that he had attended. Peg looked much more together than the last time he had seen her. She tried to open the door out but his chair was in the way. There was barely enough room on this ramp to navigate his chair to the right, and out of the way of the door, without falling off of the ramp. He then had to push the joystick quickly to the left to aim his chair through the door. It never failed that one of the handles on his chair would get hung up on the bar across the middle of the door.

Peg stepped outside to give him more room to get his chair through. "Hi, Jerry." She said. He smiled back. Each time he had gone through this door, he swore to himself that he wouldn't ever go there again. Once he was inside, Peg retreated to the table next to the window.

Jerry brought his right forearm up in front of his face and pushed the sunglasses up off his eyes and onto his forehead. He felt like people at the tables were peeking at him from behind their hamburgers and tacos.

He fished around in the bag on the side of his chair and finally clutched the note on computer paper that he had written earlier. He jammed the paper between his knees and propelled his chair over to the line of people waiting to order.

As he was waiting, a girl strolled past outside, and he felt a longing to be able to meet her and get to know her.

Finally, the person in front of him placed an order and stepped aside. He then pushed the joystick forward and moved his chair up to the order window. He grabbed the paper and placed it on the counter.

The young high school boy behind the counter was startled and wasn't sure what he should do. There was panic on the lad's face. Dealing with a handicapped person wasn't in any part of his job orientation. Soon, the manager rushed to the window and taking Jerry's note said, apologetically, "New kid, Jerry." He shouted toward the back, "Two tacos to go." Then back to Jerry, "$2.75."

Jerry held out his money bag and the man reached over the counter opening the bag and began to count out the change, "seventy-five, one dollar, one twenty-five, two, two fifty, and two seventy-five." The manager closed Jerry's bag and stuffed it back between his left leg and the side of his chair. "Can't be too careful around this neighborhood."

Jerry nodded.

"Your order will be right up." He walked away from the window shouting, "Where are those two tacos to go? This has to be the slowest fast food place in town." Jerry drove his chair a few feet to the pickup window and waited. He soon noticed a toddler becoming inquisitive about his chair. So Jerry showed the little boy how the horn worked. Jerry enjoyed showing the boy his chair but the boy's mother pulled the boy away, telling him not to bother the man.

Slowly, a high school girl came out from behind the counter with Jerry's order. He pointed to the bag attached to the back of his chair and the girl put the tacos in it.

As he headed toward the door, the manager jokingly told Jerry that he had "caused enough trouble around there for one day." Peg opened the door and Jerry drove his chair through, down the narrow ramp, and made his way toward the light at the corner.

Megan's one job and then her other.
Jerry's day off, that wasn't.
Both continue.

Chapter 3

Starting down Hunt Street, Jerry wheeled past a woman holding a sign: WILL WORK FOR FOOD. She had blond hair tied up on top of her head and wore a dirty green dress under her long brown sweater. He smiled and she grinned back. He reached into the bag that held his board and pulled out a dollar. He held it out to her and at first she didn't know what he intended, but he moved his hand closer and she took the dollar.

When Jerry came to the end of Hunt Street, he waited for the light to change and then crossed. Across the street was the Catholic Church. He always drove his chair down the driveway that only the priests used. Jerry figured, if he was hit there, he would be assured of having someone readily available to pray for his soul.

Jerry caught sight of the off-white stucco building on the church grounds where Megan took care of the preschoolers. He turned his chair around and drove back down the driveway and around the convent.

He cut through the parking lot. If it had been a Sunday, he would have been taking his life in his hands. After people go to church, they drive as if they couldn't wait to get out of there, and, if a guy was in a wheelchair, he was fair game.

Sometimes, when he went out in his chair, he felt as if people were playing, "Hit the guy in the wheelchair and get three points." He had been winning this game for ten years now. So far, nobody had won any points.

Jerry took a left at the first building and drove up the driveway. He drove his chair up to the door, where he knew Megan was watching the children, and knocked lightly. There wasn't any answer. He was pretty sure he had the right room. He knocked again. No answer. He drove around and rapped on the window.

Megan peeked out from behind the door and he wheeled back around. "Jerry, what on earth are you doing here?"

"Oh, the Pope sent me over here to straighten out some things, and I thought I'd stop and see you."

Megan pulled the door behind her leaving it ajar. "Jerry, keep your voice down. Your voice carries, when you're trying to pronounce words clearly. I just got all the kids down for their naps." Megan stepped around the corner of the building. "Is there anything wrong?"

"No, but something came for you."

"What, that form I have to sign? That isn't until next week, I thought."

"Hey, I don't know. I'm just the delivery boy. It's in the bag on the back of my chair."

Megan looked in the door, checked the room, and then dug around in his bag until she found the tacos. "Jerry, you are too much."

"You told me that you didn't have time to make lunch this morning."

"You went all the way to Jack-in-the-Box to get this for me?"

"It gave me a good reason to drive past both swimming pools and check out the women."

"One day, they are going to get wise to you." She leaned across and gave him a light kiss on the back of his neck. "It was nice of you to bring me the tacos."

"Well, I couldn't let my best aide starve."

"I had better get back in there before those kids wake up."

He placed his hand in the small of her back and just held it there. "Yeah, we don't want twenty preschoolers scurrying out into the church's parking lot."

"And they all would want a ride in your chair." Megan grinned at him, dashed back into the room, and shut the door.

Jerry clutched the joystick and whirled his chair around to the left. The door to the church was open and he steered his chair toward the ramp which, due to his suggestion, only recently had been installed.

Before that, it had taken four men to carry the wheelchair bound patients, who lived in rest homes, up the three steps each Sunday. He had always hoped that God blessed those four men. Jerry never went into the church that way, so the men never had to lift him and his chair. He used a door, on the far side, that didn't have any steps. It was not close to where the vans could drop off the people from the rest homes.

He turned his chair on the slowest speed and wheeled up the ramp and into the church. The wooden door had heavy steel around the edge so the church couldn't be broken into.

Wheeling across to the sanctuary, he asked God to look after Megan, help her with her job, and with whatever troubles she might have. Then he asked God, to help him to live alone, if that was His will. Next, he asked for help with the article that he was writing for the handicapped newsletter.

As Jerry was saying the Our Father, the priest came over and condescendingly asked if he was "being a good boy." Jerry nodded and the priest patted Jerry's head.

When the priest walked away, Jerry asked God to forgive the priest for acting as if Jerry were a child. He also prayed that someday, God would teach the priest that all handicapped people aren't retarded and shouldn't be treated that way. Jerry admitted this might be a way that God was using him, but sometimes he lost his patience. He promised God that he would keep trying.

He finished the Our Father and turned his chair toward the exit. When he reached the door, Frank held it open for him. He had known Frank, a tall man with a grayish black beard, a long time. Once, Frank had fixed a flat on Jerry's wheelchair and, from time-to-time, Jerry enjoyed driving the four blocks to Frank's house just to talk.

Ever since the company, where Frank had worked for eighteen years, had laid him off, he had been going to church every morning. This made Jerry sad. Frank followed him outside. "Don't get any speeding tickets on the way home."

Jerry turned his chair around to face him and smiled. "I'll try."

Frank grinned back and then slowly walked back into the church closing the door behind him.

Jerry drove down the driveway, hoping the old priest wouldn't decide to take his daily drive right then. The priest drove as if he was eager to meet his maker.

At the end of the driveway, Jerry looked both ways. He then thrust his control stick forward and propelled his chair across the street. He reached the other driveway just as he finished another Our Father.

At the gate to his apartment complex, he pushed a white button on the garage door opener fastened to the inside of his wheelchair, and the gate swung open. As he entered the courtyard in the center of the apartments, Linda came bounding down the stairs of her apartment.

Linda wasn't like most of the people living in low-income housing in that she had not been defeated and actively worked on improving her situation. Linda was going to school to be a psych technician, while caring for her nine-year-old daughter. "Hey Jerry, have you been out terrorizing the neighborhood again?"

He guided his chair over to her stairs. "I have to do something for fun."

She hurried down the last couple of steps. "I have to pick up my kid from school. I thought you went to The Center today?"

Jerry pulled out his letter board from the bag, on the left side of his wheelchair, to spell out words, while conversing with Linda. "I d-e-c-i-d-e-d to work on the article at home and t-a-k-e it into The Center tomorrow."

"Waiting until the last minute, I see."

"Look who's t-a-l-k-i-n-g. You do your essays at three in the morning on the days that they are due."

"Thank God, most of those days are over."

"If it hadn't taken you a whole year to speak to me, maybe I could have helped you sooner!"

"Gee, Jerry, you aren't going to let me live that one down, are you?"

"And you were studying how to work with people who had special needs."

"Well, you didn't look like anyone who had any special needs. Besides, you didn't make any particular effort to communicate with me."

"Well . . ."

"As a matter of fact, didn't you write in one article how disabled people need to make an extra effort to communicate?"

"Now, that was different. That was for the

newsletter."

"Shouldn't you practice what you preach?"

"Occasionally." Jerry replied.

She chuckled. "It only took me fifteen minutes to figure out that you wanted me to pick up your sunglasses."

"And, you thought I was going to hit you w-i-t-h my communication board, the first time I pulled it out."

"Hey, I had never seen one of those things before. They never told us about those things at school. All I saw was this man coming at me with this wooden object."

"Didn't your daughter figure out what my board was?"

She thought a minute. "That's right. It's neat how kids don't have any pre-conceived ideas about people, like adults do."

"Yes."

"Speaking of kids, I had better go get my brat before she disowns me." She started walking toward the carport. "I'll be up tonight, if you need anything."

"Another class?"

"You guessed it." She continued out to her car.

He turned his joystick and pointed his chair towards his apartment door. Jerry was glad that Craig was not around right then, since he had forgotten to pick up something for Craig at the store. It was always painful to admit to a child his age that you had not done something you had promised him you would do.

He steered his chair up the wooden ramp and let go of his control stick. After his chair automatically locked in place, he reached inside the bag on the side of his chair and pulled out the long aluminum tube. There was a spring on the end of the tube attached to his door key. He slipped the tube into another pipe fastened to his door and guided the key into the lock. He turned the tube inside the pipe, which unlocked his door.

Inside, he transferred to his manual chair, wheeled himself backward into his computer room, and started working on the article for the newsletter.

Megan's surprise.
Megan's other job.
Just another day for Jerry.

Chapter 4

The walls inside the church's preschool were painted
a light green. There was a large mural, of round-faced
boys and girls carrying lunch pails and schoolbooks,
wrapped around the room. One part of the mural covered
a window frame, so half of one boy's face was molded
into the window framework.

Megan wove her way through the sea of active
preschoolers while shouting, "Ten more minutes before
your parents come! Get your backpacks and papers from
the shelf." Along one wall were wooden boxes where
children's belongings were stored during the day.

All forty kids scampered at once toward the wooden
boxes. "One at a time, please." Megan made her way
through the ocean of arms and legs to place some scissors
in a desk drawer.

As Megan closed the drawer, Toby, who was not quite
four, sauntered up to Megan. "Miss Megan?"

"Yes, Toby?"

"I have been good all day. Please make a ship for me,
you promised."

"Why, yes I did, didn't I?"

Toby nodded, and Megan reached into the drawer and

pulled out the scissors.

"Don't tell the others. This is just for you."

Toby got nearer and watched closely as Megan pulled out some paper and began to fashion a ship out of it, and then colored it with crayons. Megan gave the paper ship to Toby.

"Thank you, Miss Megan."

"Remember, Toby, just this time." Megan reached for Toby's jacket to help put it on.

"I'll remember, Miss Megan," Toby said.

Megan finished helping Toby on with his jacket and he dashed out the door and climbed into one of the waiting automobiles. She watched until the last child had gone, then picked up all the toys, and put them away. Finally, she locked up the church day care and walked across the street.

She reached the gate to Jerry's apartment complex. She started to search for the key on her ring, then stopped when she noticed that the lock had been broken again. She was concerned about Jerry living there alone with such a lack of security.

Just as Megan entered the gate, Vanessa, one of the children from the day care center said, "Hello, Miss Megan, what are you doing here?"

"Oh, hi, Vanessa. I came to see a friend."

"Jerry?" Vanessa inquired.

"Why, yes."

"The man in the wheelchair?"

"That's right," replied Megan. She continued walking past the barracks-like apartment buildings.

"Does he sleep in that chair?"

"No, Vanessa."

"Then, where does he sleep?" Vanessa inquisitively pleaded.

"In a bed, just like you and me," said Megan.

"Oh." Vanessa thought a moment and then went over to her friends and resumed playing.

Megan walked on to Jerry's apartment. She inserted the key into the door and was surprised to find the door unlocked. She opened the door and entered, shutting the door behind her. Jerry's chair wasn't in its usual place and Jerry's coat lay in the middle of the living room.

Megan walked down the hall. Jerry was using words that she seldom heard him say. She peeped around the bedroom door.

Jerry stood up, holding the bathroom bar with his right hand, while pulling down on his pants with his left hand. But, the pants wouldn't budge. He tried pulling down at the right side of his pants again and then the left and kept alternating back and forth. He used more of the language she had heard earlier. She could tell he was frustrated and angry. He pulled one more time with his left hand and his pants and underwear inched down a little bit more.

After his pants were just below his rear, he sat down and pushed them down his legs until they were down below his knees. They wouldn't go over his shoes, so he pulled them back up so he could work each pant leg over one shoe at a time. The left pant leg became caught on his shoe. He muttered more frustrated language.

He straightened the pant leg out and then reached down to push the material over the heel of his shoe. Then, with his right foot holding down his pants, he pulled his left foot out of the wet tangle of underwear and pants. Next, he held the pants down with his left foot, while he pulled his right leg out.

The underwear was stuck on the toe of his shoe. So, he reached down and snatched the wet underwear. Then, holding it as far away from his face as his jerkiness would allow, he moved his chair towards the dirty clothes basket. When it seemed that his hand was right over the basket, he let go. He missed. He muttered another obviously unprintable word.

"What kind of language is that?" Megan laughed.

Jerry jerked around and looked toward Megan standing in the bedroom doorway. "How long have you been there?"

Megan came across and started helping Jerry change into a pair of sweat pants that he had already retrieved from the closet. "Long enough to hear some real fancy words."

"You spy." Jerry wheeled over and held onto the bar next to the shower stall.

"Not me. I'm innocent. But, I don't know about your

language. Maybe, The Center is right in not letting you work with young disabled people. No telling what you might teach them."

Jerry held onto the bar and stood up. "Come on, Megan, give me some slack."

She pulled his sweats on over his shoes and helped him back into his chair. "All right. How did you get into this mess?"

"I had the day off and decided to go to the movies. I thought I could make it home in time to go to the bathroom. I didn't." Jerry sat down.

Megan picked up his wet clothes and hung them across the bar in the bathroom. "I thought you had friends at the theater who helped you."

With his pants still down around his ankles, Jerry turned so Megan could wipe off his legs and front. "The doorman, who knows me, wasn't working, and I couldn't find the usher that I know."

Megan then helped pull up his pants the rest of the way. "You told me once that you would ask a girl to help you before you would ask a boy."

"Yes, somehow I feel more comfortable asking a woman."

"Is it from the time you were living in the care facility years ago?" Megan finished dressing Jerry and wheeled him out into the bedroom.

"I don't think that is entirely the reason."

"Could it be that women are thought of as nurses as a

rule?"

"I hadn't ever thought of it that way, but you could be right, I guess." When they reached the living room, Jerry started pushing himself with his feet. "I'm glad that I caught you before you left home this morning."

"I was just headed out. You didn't say why you needed me today." Megan picked up Jerry's jacket and placed it across the arm of the couch, where Jerry could reach it if he needed it.

"Evelyn called me last night and said she was sick but I know she had too much to drink. She tied on a good one and needed the whole day to sleep it off."

Megan walked into the kitchen. "Maybe Evelyn was really sick." Megan remembered that Rick had asked her to call in sick for him more and more in the last month.

"Girl, we have both been down that road. I know what's happening by the tone of her voice." He wheeled up to the table.

"Well, at least I always made it to work the next day. Evelyn doesn't have to be here until four in the afternoon. I dragged my ass over here at seven o'clock in the stupid morning after partying until three."

Jerry replied, chuckling. "I know and I always made it to school. I'm afraid that Evelyn has deeper problems than we both had."

"Want some of this fish and potatoes with green beans?"

"Bring on the food, woman." Jerry licked his lips.

"Okay, hungry man. Jerry, what do you mean about Evelyn?"

"Well, Megan, we both admitted that we had a problem."

Megan started frying the fish and potatoes. "Yes, I know that's the first step, and it's the hardest."

"Some need to attend AA meetings and some are able to do it on their own. Those potatoes smell delicious."

"Rick has missed his last four meetings."

"Has he started drinking again?" Jerry nervously put paper towels, which he used as napkins, on the table. "Are you all right?"

Megan didn't say anything for several minutes and then she began to sob. "Rick keeps asking me to go out drinking with him." Jerry wheeled around the table and over to Megan and reached out both arms. Megan knelt, allowing Jerry to place his arms around her neck. "I love Rick so much."

Jerry pressed his cheek to Megan's wet face. "I know."

She rose slowly to her feet. "I got tears in your food."

Jerry rolled his chair back to the table. "Does that mean I have to pay you more?"

"Of course." She dished up the food and brought it over to the table. "Best tear-covered food you've ever eaten." Megan started cutting up Jerry's food with a knife. "I'm not going to use the food processor tonight. You need to use the muscles in your mouth and throat."

"How did you know that?"

"You told me."

"Oh yes, I did, didn't I" She gave Jerry his first bite. As Jerry was chewing, she asked, "Do you think you'll be all right with Evelyn?"

"I've already paid her for this month and . . . "

She dropped the spoon. "Jerry! You knew the woman had a drinking problem and you paid her in advance. Not very smart! Not very smart at all."

"I just wanted to give her a chance." He opened his mouth for the next bite.

"I should shove this spoon down your throat. You're too nice."

He chewed up the bite and swallowed. "You help Rick."

"Rick is in recovery, Evelyn isn't." She began cutting up the fish. "Be careful, this bite is kind of big."

"Okay" He took the bite and chewed the best he could. "But you said that Rick isn't going to the meetings."

"I'm not letting Rick's behavior affect me. If you hadn't given Evelyn the advance, she might not have gone out drinking. And then maybe, she wouldn't have called in sick and you wouldn't have had to call me."

He swallowed. "I'm sorry I needed to call."

"Jerry, I told you to call anytime you needed me. The point is that, if you had not given Evelyn the advance, you wouldn't have had to call anyone. Can't you see that?"

"Maybe I didn't use my best judgment. That isn't any reason to jump all over me."

She placed an arm around his shoulders. "If you didn't mean so much to me, I wouldn't talk this way. People always seem to take advantage of you and your situation."

He cleaned his mouth. "I know it, but I don't want to be suspicious of everyone I hire."

"I know, but I just get angry each time you get hurt."

"But where would I be if I didn't keep trying?"

"I agree but I can't stop worrying." She scraped all the food to one side of the plate. "There are about three more bites. Want them?"

"Sure. Where did you learn to be such a good cook? I remember the first time you fixed dinner for me. You didn't know how to make macaroni and cheese from a box." Jerry opened his mouth.

"Didn't you think I would improve with age?" She gave him the bite.

He chewed and swallowed. "I was hoping you would, or I was going to have to go on a strict diet."

"You're mean. Why do I stand for this abuse?" She readied the spoon with the next bite.

"You know you love it."

"I should stick this spoon all the way down to your toes. Open up, Old Man."

"You wouldn't do that. I haven't paid you yet this

month."

"With my luck, you won't have enough. You already gave all your money to Evelyn."

"That isn't fair."

She grinned. "I stopped playing fair with you a long time ago but you never knew it, Old Man."

"You should respect your elders."

"You're right. People your age can't help being dim-witted. Here, take the last bite of this delicious feast I made for you." She held the spoon up to his lips.

"You are getting testy." He opened his mouth, taking the last bite.

"I started work this morning at six, spent two hours here with an annoying but lovable old man, and I still have to go to my AA meeting."

"Annoying but lovable?"

"Yes, that describes you pretty well." She grinned as she cleared the table.

"That was a good dinner." He helped throw away the used paper towels. "I hope I haven't made you late for your meeting."

"Nah. I have lots of time. If it weren't for Rick, I would probably skip the meeting. I have ten pages of math tonight."

"Oh, I want my western shirt on before you leave." He picked up the dishrag and started to wipe off the table.

She took the rag. "Here, I'll do that. Western shirt?

You've already been out once today."

Jerry wheeled down the hall toward his bedroom. "Betty is dropping by tonight."

"Betty?" She bustled after him. "Who's Betty?"

He wheeled over to the closet. "She is someone I met through an electronic bulletin board on my computer."

She walked over to help him put on the western shirt. "Tell me about Betty." Megan pulled off his T-shirt and wiped his chest down.

"Betty works as a secretary for the school district and enjoys playing chess. She has come over twice and wants to come back. That's just as much as I know."

Megan helped him on with the shirt. "Maybe that's all you need to know for now." She straightened the shirt and combed his black, gray-streaked hair over to the left side. She took two steps backwards. "What a hunk." She turned around, waved good-bye over her shoulder, and then ran down the hall.

Jerry heard the front door open and shut. He turned and looked in the mirror. "Hunk?"

Jerry's day begins.
Megan's troubles begin.
A friendship is shown.

Chapter 5

As the warm shower water washed down over Jerry's head and body, he realized this was the only time he was completely alone. The rest of the day, he needed aides or friends to help him. Even though he knew Megan was just on the other side of the shower curtain, he felt some privacy for this short while.

He remembered a time when he hadn't had this much privacy. Every third morning in the hospital, at ten o'clock, the same five men had been taken into the large bathroom and stripped. There had been just one tub and one aide had given all the baths. Sometimes, one aide had peeled off their clothes, while the other had washed everyone. One by one, the aides had lifted them into the warm water.

When a young female aide had been on bath duty, he hadn't known whom he felt more embarrassed for, her, or himself. He just had to lie there and the aide had to do her job. He hadn't been an individual; he had been just another body to wash. He had thought of the outdoors or had replayed in his mind a TV program that he had seen the night before.

Barbara, an older aide, had talked about what had

happened in the news or the baseball game to make the bath time seem to pass faster. The patients had liked it, when Barbara had bath duty.

Jerry heard Megan straightening up the bottles of baby oil and after-shave by the sink. "I'm ready," he called.

"Just a second," Megan said.

He heard her set the bottles and the hairbrush back on the sink. She reached through the shower curtain and turned off the water. "Sorry to take so long, but your sink area was a mess. I couldn't stand it any longer."

She dried him with a towel and then he stood up holding onto the bar. She steadied him around the waist and he stepped over the lip of the shower. She quickly put a towel in the seat of his wheelchair. "Boy, I almost forgot the towel." She then proceeded to dry his legs.

"You remembered in time, you don't lose any points." He held up his right leg so she could dry his foot.

"I didn't know this was a point system." Megan said.

"I just made it up." He held up his left leg.

"You didn't tell me." She laid his leg across her lap to dry it. He jumped when the phone rang. "Easy."

"That startle reflex gets me every time." He pulled himself back into his chair.

Megan threw a towel over his lap and walked across to answer the speaker phone. "Hello, Jerry's place."

"Hey!"

"Rick?" Megan's face was strained.

"I need five dollars. I'll meet you by the gate," Rick demanded.

"I don't have it. I told you not to call me at work." She leaned against the bed.

"You are just there with Jerry. You said Jerry is like a friend."

"Yes, but I'm giving him his care right now. He has things to do and he can't start before I finish getting him ready," Megan explained.

"Take me off the squawk box." This was what Rick called Jerry's speaker phone.

She picked up the receiver. "I don't have it. What happened to the money that was on the table?" She listened for a second. "I thought you were going to use that for food." Then, she spoke harshly. "You shouldn't have spent that money on your friends. I have to get back to work." She slammed down the phone. She came marching back to where Jerry was sitting.

"Down girl . . . I'm a friend," Jerry said.

She giggled. "Don't worry. You're safe. As for the man I live with . . ." She pulled up Jerry's pants and started putting on his shirt.

"Trouble in paradise?" Jerry asked.

She struggled with his right arm putting it into the shirt. "It figures that your right arm would be difficult today. Try to relax."

"Okay." Because he felt Megan was upset, his body was reacting to what was going on around him.

Then the shirt slipped right on. "Well, things are looking up. I don't have to break your arm today after all. Jerry, it looks like Rick spent all our food money at that bar last night. He called needing gas money to get to work."

Jerry stood up by the bar in the bathroom so she could straighten his clothes. "I have some money."

"No Jerry, I put some money away. I thought he might pull something like this."

"I thought Rick had been doing better the past few weeks." Jerry sat back into his chair.

Megan came around in front of his chair to put on his socks and shoes. "He had been doing all right for a while, and then things started going bad at work. After that, he seemed to lose interest in everything."

"Everything?"

She struggled with his right shoe. "Yes, everything. His job, his painting, the AA program, and me."

"I didn't know things had gotten that bad."

"I wanted to keep it to myself. I was hoping things would get better." She tied his shoes.

Jerry bent down and squeezed her right shoulder. "I'm sorry."

"I guess I just have to let Rick do whatever he is going to do. I've been keeping busy, getting ready for my next class. It's in child development. I've already taken the first part. I heard the second part is really a bear."

He straightened up in his chair. "I wish I could do

more for you. You do so much for me."

"Jerry, you do a lot just listening to all my problems."

He looked into the mirror. "I don't like this shirt."

"What's wrong with it? You chose it. You're just going to be working at home today."

"I want a different shirt. There's one in the second drawer."

Megan opened the second drawer and there was a red and blue package with her name on it. "What is this?"

Jerry laughed. "Did you find my shirt?"

She replied, "There's a package with my name on it."

"Then, it must be for you."

"But, what is it?"

"Open it."

"Is it really for me?"

"Yes."

Megan became like a little girl while she opened the package, tearing the paper. "It's the book I need for that class!" she exclaimed in happy puzzlement.

"You said that you didn't know how you were going to have enough money to buy it."

"Jerry. Thanks." She gazed at the book and started to reach down to hug him. "That dumb chair."

Suddenly she picked him up out of his chair and held him against her body to hug him. He put both arms around her and held her for a long time. He couldn't remember hugging anyone this way before. It felt good. "Thank you for the book," she whispered.

"You're welcome. You have your hair in my mouth."

"What?" She sat him back in his chair and looked into the mirror. She pulled saliva out of her hair. "How did you know which book?"

"I asked a teacher I know."

She took a cloth and wiped his lips. "You're pretty sneaky."

"Only when I have to be." He commenced wheeling out of his bedroom and into the room where his computer was set up.

"I'll get your drinks," she called after him. A few minutes later, she walked down the hall carrying three glasses: one with coffee, one with water, and one with prune juice.

"Don't forget to drink your prune juice. I don't want to have to give you an enema."

"Oh, believe me, that is the last thing I want you to do."

"Hey!" she said abruptly.

"What?"

"Thanks for the book." She smiled. "See you tomorrow at eight."

Jerry's happiness,
Is swept away,
By Megan's sadness.

Chapter 6

Jerry was sitting at the kitchen table. He took another sip of his coffee. The door opened behind him. Megan said, "Jerry, what are you doing up this early?"

Jerry turned his chair. He just had on a pair of shorts. "Betty and I went to the show. We got back late so she stayed here. We got up early so she could go home to get ready for work."

Megan locked the front door. "My, my."

Grinning, he turned to eye Megan.

Megan said, "You haven't mentioned her for a long time. I was wondering about her. Want breakfast?"

"Just eggs and toast. I didn't want to say anything before Betty and I worked things out." He sipped his coffee.

She walked past him. "I can't really blame you, after how Anne just left."

"Yes, Anne did a number on me. Just disappearing."

"I was worried about you back then," said Megan, looking for the eggs and bread in the refrigerator.

"You had reason to be. I had been off the hard stuff only three months, when Anne just packed up and moved."

Megan began cooking. "Anne sure was strange. She bought that house, saying that she wanted you to move in with her. Then, out of the blue, she moved to who knows where."

"She suddenly realized what it would be like living with someone who has a handicap."

"Come on, Jerry. You two went together almost three years and then your handicap, all of a sudden, became an issue?" She imagined Jerry would be easy to live with, compared to Rick. She felt herself becoming jealous of Betty.

"Well, like you said, Anne was a strange character."

Megan brought a plate over to the table and started to feed Jerry. "Betty seems nice. What does she look like?"

Jerry swallowed his food. "Well, she is about my age, a little over five feet tall, and has brown, graying hair."

"I'm happy you have met someone," she said. "Here, eat your eggs." Megan put milk over his toast, to soften it a bit so he could swallow it without choking. "It must have been hard to reach out again."

"Yes, but I guess I just got tired of talking to these walls."

Megan smiled. "If you have had any conversations with walls, you have serious problems."

"Oh, I don't know, talking to walls and talking to you are about the same." Jerry smiled, taking his next mouthful.

"You're full of it this morning." She stood and slowly

walked across to the sink. She started to wash the dishes then suddenly burst into tears.

Alarmed, Jerry cleaned his mouth and carefully placed the napkin down on the table. He pushed away from his place, forcing the wheels over the hump that separated the dining room from the kitchen. As he approached her, he reached for her hand. "What's wrong?"

"Oh, it's just that I fixed a nice dinner for Rick, I cleaned the apartment, and I wore my kimono. . ." She tried to continue. Jerry took her hand and led her to a kitchen chair. She sat down, holding his hand firmly. "Rick was just interested in a baseball game on TV and then going to play pool with the guys. When he first came in, he seemed excited about everything. Then, it changed. I wasn't. . ."

Jerry held her close while she sobbed on his shoulder. "Megan, it's all right." He handed her a box of tissues.

"I thought I was all right." She wiped her nose. "I'm glad about you and Betty anyway." She gave him a hug. "Want to get dressed?"

"Yes."

She took him into the bedroom and over to the dressing area in front of the basin. "So, things still aren't any better between you and Rick?"

"Jerry, Rick just comes home to eat and sleep. No offense, I feel like an aide to both you and Rick."

"So, the special dinner didn't help?"

"No."

"I want to wear that blue tank top. So, how much is Rick still hanging around with his drinking buddies?"

"I don't know. With school and two jobs, I hardly have time for myself. I thought we would spend more time together when classes ended." She rushed through her work. "Your reading glasses are clean. Need anything else?"

"No. Thanks."

"Thanks for listening and I'm really happy about you and Betty. See you tomorrow at eight." She started toward the door.

"Megan."

"What?"

"How short is your kimono?"

"You'll never know."

"I might want to buy Betty one."

"Then schedule a bus ride to the mall."

"You could model it."

"Dream on."

Jerry ponders why.
Betty,
Is Jerry's relief.

Chapter 7

Jerry's bedroom was dark, except for the blue light on the front of his radio. The blues song could hardly be heard. Jerry was lying with his shirt and tie still fastened. He opened his eyes and gazed at the light streaming through the beige slats of the blinds. Was it dawn or dusk? Then he remembered coming home from another interview. It had been a nightmare. When he got home, he had just wanted to sleep.

He had told Barbara, his evening aide, to leave some chocolate milk in the refrigerator. It was in the wooden cup-holder that his friend, Marvin, had built for him, so he could get a cold drink when he was there alone. He felt the tie around his neck and wished that he had asked Barbara to take it off before she left.

He thought of turning over to turn off the radio, but merely laid there instead. He wished the darkness could swallow him and he could float away somewhere, anywhere. He wanted no more people, interviews, or bus drivers who couldn't understand him. And, he wanted no more ramps that he couldn't find. Or aides who came late or didn't come at all. No more forms from the government to sign, just to get the bare necessities. No more, no more.

The phone rang once, twice, three times before the answering machine picked it up. "Hi sweetie, I have to work late. Penny did a whole report wrong so I have to re-type it. What a nincompoop. Hope your interview went well. I'll be home by eight. Call me." He grinned.

He pulled at his tie again. Rodney, Craig's older brother, would be playing football soon, with the other kids, just outside Jerry's front door. He could get Rodney or one of the others to help him with his tie.

Jerry swung his feet off the bed. He grabbed the bar next to him and pulled himself up into a sitting position. He remained there a moment and wondered why. Why did he put himself through things like trying to get a job, rather than just staying home, or living in an institution?

He got into his chair and made his way down the hall. When he reached the living room, he noticed Barbara had broken up a candy bar and left it on the table. This enabled him to pick up the pieces with his mouth.

He opened his front door. "Rodney, come here. Rodney. Rodney."

Rodney yelled, "Time!" He threw down the football and lumbered over to Jerry's door. "What now? It's third down and one to go."

"Undo this tie."

Rodney started untying Jerry's tie. "Where's Betty?"

"She's not here."

"Call her. It's not good for a man to be alone."

Jerry thought, for an eleven-year old, Rodney had become quite a philosopher. "Thanks."

"Now, watch me make this first down." Rodney ran back to where the other kids were waiting.

Jerry watched the kids play for a while and then closed the door. He wheeled back into his bedroom and pulled the white shirt off over his head. As he pulled his right arm out of his sleeve, he heard his front door open.

"Are you decent?" Megan yelled.

"This is as good as it gets!" he hollered back.

Megan ambled down the hall. She had on jeans, a black leather jacket, a T-shirt with a picture of a lion on the front, and in her left hand was a bag of French fries. "New style of wearing your shirt, one sleeve on and the other one off? Nice touch."

"Aren't you going to help?"

"No. You gave me three days off, and I'm going to take full advantage of it. Actually, something must be terribly wrong with me that I'm here at all."

"Megan, I didn't get the stupid job."

"Oh, I'm sorry." Megan flopped down on Jerry's bed. "I'm still not going to help you."

He swore under his breath and struggled with the shirt. He put a foot on one sleeve while he jerked his arm out of the other sleeve. "Happy now?"

"Like a pig in mud." She popped a French fry in her mouth. "I'd offer you one of these fries but they're hard and you could get it caught in your throat. I don't want to spend my day off in an emergency room with you. Selfish broad, aren't I?"

"That's one of many adjectives that I could use to describe you right now." He threw his shirt in the dirty clothes basket.

"Rick could probably help think up a lot more. Now, I thought that job was in the bag."

He was sweating. "It was, until they discovered I can't read," he said in a quiet tone.

She sat straight up on the bed. "But you wrote a million short stories, articles, not to mention that novel you did in school."

"I know." He cleared his throat. "I can see in my mind how something should look on paper and I kind of recreate it on my computer."

"And for school?"

"I can remember what I hear. In college, I got books on tape, like the blind students. I said that I couldn't turn pages."

"You didn't really lie." She found a soft middle of a French fry and placed it in his mouth. "Let it melt in your mouth. What about taking notes?"

"Instructors let me tape the lectures and at home. . ."

"What about in grade school?"

"Remember, my speech defect was much worse then. When I didn't know a word, I faked the teachers out. See what a deceitful idiot I am."

"Jerry, you're a genius." She was excited.

"What?"

"You overcame a handicap people didn't know you had. That takes a creative mind. You're a genius, I tell you."

He slipped off his pants and sat there in his underwear. "I usually don't entertain guests in this attire. I never thought of my reading problem that way."

"You learned to do it because you didn't want to be left behind and had the brains to find a way around the problem. I really admire you for that."

"I still feel embarrassed about not being able to read." He threw his black coat in the direction of the shelf."

"Don't." She threw the paper bag away. Then she walked over and hung up the coat.

"I thought you said that you were off work."

"Betty paid good money for it. And you have Dick for the next two mornings. I'm sure, if I left it on the floor, that coat would still be there when I come back in two days."

"I can't believe Dick is going to nursing school."

"He sure is a slob. It's a good thing you have Betty. She truly cares for you."

"I know." He looked at the picture on the nightstand. "This was taken soon after we met."

"Gee, Rick never looks at my picture wearing just his underwear. I'm jealous."

"Speaking of the old fellow, what's going to happen when you get home?"

"Don't know and don't care. There's this hunk at the AA meeting who has asked me out for coffee afterwards."

Jerry playfully flexed his arm muscles. "Is he as brawny as this?" She thought how cute Jerry looked right then.

"I might let you know." She walked past Jerry's answering machine. "You have a call."

"It's Betty."

"It looks like we both have some business to attend to," she said smiling.

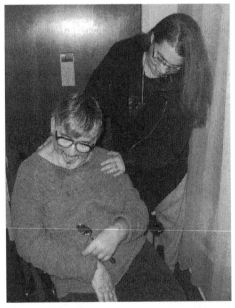

Spoon in hand and ready for dinner.

Jerry's trip to the mall.
Some challenges.
But Betty was worth it.

Chapter 8

Jerry searched the computer directories and files for the partially prepared note and brought it up on the screen. Then he added the necessary information.

Hello,
　My name is Jerry and I have cerebral palsy. Even though I have a speech defect, I comprehend everything. If you can't understand me, I'll spell words out on my letter board.
　I would like to purchase a kimono.
　Thank you very much,
Jerry

He first ran the spell-check program and then activated the print command. He put down his typing stick and wheeled across to the printer. He pulled off the page but it ripped. "It figures. Ten minutes before my bus comes," he muttered to himself.

He threw the paper into the wastebasket, wheeled back to the keyboard, picked up his typing stick, and executed the print command again. He slammed down his typing stick, rushed back to the printer, moved the paper up to the fold, took hold of the paper, and tore off the page. Only a small piece at the bottom was missing; otherwise, the message was intact. It would have to do. He wheeled into the living room, folded the note, and stuffed it into the bag on the side of his electric wheelchair.

He wheeled across to the sofa where his jacket was lying. He first put his right arm through the right sleeve. Then grabbed the bottom of the jacket in his right hand, holding onto it, so he could shove his left arm through the other sleeve. Then, with both hands, he pulled the jacket over his head.

He glanced in the mirror on his way back across the room. His hair was a mess. "The rugged look today," he thought, as he wheeled to his power wheelchair. He grabbed the bar on the wall, stood up, swung over, and sat in his electric wheelchair. He switched it on and guided it with the control stick toward the front door. He then went through his usual maneuvers to get out the door and lock it.

He needed his seat belt fastened but he remembered that Craig and the other older kids were not out of school yet. There were two preschoolers playing in the courtyard, so he guided his chair over to them. The boy and girl ran toward him. He pointed to his seat belt.

"He wants his seat belt on," the girl said.

"I know," replied the little boy.

"Then help him," said the girl, putting a thoughtful

finger in her mouth.

"I don't know how," stated the little boy.

Jerry brought both ends of the seat belt as close together as he could. "That's how," the girl explained.

The boy straddled Jerry's legs and tried to fasten the seat belt. "I can't."

"Try harder," the girl said. "He might fall out and get hurt."

The boy tried twice more without success. Then a teenager walked past and Jerry motioned to him. He strolled over and fastened the seat belt. "Later, Jerry," he said as he ran up one of the stairwells.

The two youngsters went back to playing. "See that's how you do it," the girl said.

Jerry wheeled past the two children and steered his chair down the walkway to the carport area. Then he drove across the place in the asphalt in front of the automatic gate. He knew the weight of his power wheelchair should trigger the automatic gate opener. The gate worked today, which surprised Jerry.

The special bus for seniors and disabled people was waiting for Jerry. "Hi, Jerry," called Juan, the driver.

Jerry drove his wheelchair along the side of the bus as Juan stepped down the four steps and opened the two wide doors on the side of the bus. "Hey, Juan, I haven't seen you in a while."

Juan lowered the lift, which was made of steel with crisscrossed raised areas so it wouldn't be slippery when someone drove a wheelchair onto it. "I've been on nights."

Jerry backed his chair onto the lift. "I wondered where you were."

"School in the days and driving at night. Take the space behind the driver's seat. I have to keep an eye on you." Juan pushed a black button that automatically raised the lift to the level of the bus floor. "Watch my feet," Juan said stepping back.

"You take all the fun out of getting on this bus." Jerry slowly guided his chair inside.

"Not bad." Juan tapped the joystick moving the chair slightly to the right. "Just a minor adjustment." Then, he wrapped four straps around the sides of Jerry's chair and snapped the other ends of the straps into the floor slot. He moved the chair back and forth. "That baby isn't going anywhere."

He then brought the seatbelt around Jerry. He put up the lift to its vertical position, went outside to close the doors, walked up the steps, and climbed into the driver's seat. "Well, are you going shopping or just planning to check out the girls?" Juan joked with Jerry, as they drove toward the mall.

"Who me?" Jerry said innocently, while he thumbed around in his bag for the coupons needed to pay for his ride. The state issued him ten coupons each month. They didn't want passengers to carry money on these buses. However, most people taking these buses usually had money for shopping, which was the main purpose for the bus service. It didn't make much sense.

"Don't play that innocent act with me. I saw you checking out the chicks, the last time I dropped you at the mall. Hey, check out the one on the corner."

Jerry had to lean forward to see out the front window. The way the bus was set up, passengers in wheelchairs had a limited view out the side windows. "Drive around the block again. That doesn't look too bad."

"You fool. I'm not going to miss my lunch break, just so you can check out chicks." A little while later, Juan pulled into the parking lot of the mall and parked by the entrance. "Get off my bus you dirty old man." He started untying the wheelchair.

"It takes one to know one." Jerry held out the coupon.

Juan grabbed the coupon. "Paper money to boot. Get off my bus right now." He teased Jerry while undoing all the safety straps. He positioned the lift and Jerry drove his chair onto it. After lowering him to the sidewalk, Juan placed a hand on Jerry's shoulder. "Take it easy, man."

"You too."

Jerry drove his chair toward the automatic doors at the mall entrance. Just inside the doors, there was a wall mirror. Jerry reached behind his head and stuck his thumb into the cloth strap, which held on his dark glasses. He pulled his dark glasses off over his head and hung them around the joystick box on the left side of his wheelchair.

He glanced into the mirror. His hair wasn't too messed up. He looked across to the other side of the mall where an art gallery was. An elderly couple was standing studying the paintings. Jerry guided his chair across to admire the paintings. As soon as he pulled up beside the couple, they hurried on their way. Wheelchairs were just too strange for some.

Inside a little room, off from the gallery, there was a man painstakingly touching up a tiny spot on a painting of a mountain range. The man noticed Jerry watching him and nodded in greeting. Jerry nodded back; as he did each trip he took to the mall. Jerry wanted to comment on the artwork and a thousand questions rushed through his mind. Sometimes a nod was all a situation would allow though.

In a few seconds, Jerry turned his chair and traveled down the right side of the mall. As he passed the toy store, he noticed a small boy with his nose pressed to the glass gazing at a building kit. When Jerry got close to the boy, Jerry stopped his wheelchair. The youngster glanced at him then came and placed a hand on Jerry's knee. Jerry smiled. The boy then ambled back to the shop window and continued his investigation of the kit.

Jerry wheeled on down past the movie theater. The man taking tickets waved and Jerry returned the greeting. Fred had helped him from time-to-time in using the restroom. Despite opposite opinions at The Center for the disabled, Jerry had found that most people were willing to help, once someone taught them. Fred walked over to Jerry. "Going to the show today?"

"Maybe later."

"Okay, just let me know, if you need any help."

"I will," Jerry said. Fred rushed back to take tickets from people waiting at the theater entrance. Jerry had important business to tend to, Betty's kimono.

Jerry turned the corner where there was a bookstore. There were exhibits of paperbacks in cardboard stands jutting out into the walkway. He almost hit one of these displays, but he jerked the joystick to the left just in time to miss bashing it. He sat there contemplating how pleasing it would be to have a novel that he had written sitting in one of those stands.

A young woman suddenly appeared in front of Jerry. She yelled, "HELLO." She was wearing white shorts and a green loose fitting blouse. "HOW ARE YOU?"

Jerry nodded. I can hear lady, he thought to himself. He didn't even try to explain.

She bent over right in front of Jerry. "ARE YOU LOST?"

He shook his head.

"ALL RIGHT, I HAVE TO GO." She walked away. He turned his chair around. Betty's kimono. He had to take care of business. He pointed his chair toward the Sears sign.

He passed through the appliance department. Again, displays obstructed his path. He pretended he was a racecar driver who had to make all those tricky turns. Three years at this mall and he hadn't broken anything yet. He had to uphold his record.

He was about to speed through the electronics department. Don, the computer salesman, shouted. "This isn't a race track." Don was tall with blond hair and blue eyes and wore a suit and tie. He pulled up a computer chair and sat down, so he would be at Jerry's eye level. "Well, how are things at The Center?"

Jerry guided his chair onto the red carpet where the demonstration computers were set up. He pulled out his letter board. Don held the board steady and glanced at it whenever Jerry motioned to it. "I don't go there much now."

"Why?"

"It has changed its focus to brain-injured individuals. Actually, I was sorry that you donated that hundred dollars."

"Well, that money went to help someone. Anyway, it was the store's money, not mine."

"That's one way to look at it. Next time, donate it to me." Jerry laughed.

"Yeah, I know what you mean. My wife and I could really use an extra hundred. My diabetes flared up and I was off a week."

"Are you all right?"

"Yeah, I just ate something I shouldn't have. That's all."

"I'm glad you're better."

"Thanks. Need any diskettes?" Don asked.

"Not this time."

"I'd better get back to work."

"See you next time." Jerry backed his chair up and headed toward the elevator.

When the doors opened, there was a lady with a baby carriage, who was leaving the elevator, so Jerry moved back. Instead of coming out, however, she held the elevator open until he could drive inside. He thanked her.

Jerry realized he was in a freight elevator and recalled a guy in a wheelchair who wouldn't use an elevator meant for merchandise. He wouldn't use a ramp behind a restaurant either, because he wanted to be treated equally. Jerry thought it was selfish and narrow minded to expect every business to be setup for wheelchairs. Wheelchairs weren't normal. Jerry moved his chair back and forth as the elevator moved downward. It was the cheapest amusement park ride in town.

The doors opened and Jerry guided his chair out of the elevator and right into the women's clothing department. He passed several large round racks where women's shirts were hanging. He touched one that had pictures of cats across the front of it. Betty would have liked something like that. A saleslady came up to him. "Can I help you, sir?"

Jerry handed her his note and waited for her to read it. Even though this was the best method to communicate with strangers, he always became anxious and nervous waiting for someone to read a note. What if he had misspelled a word or left one out?

"Right this way, Jerry." He followed the lady going right and then left between the clothes racks. She really wasn't walking fast, but it seemed so because she knew the store so well. He was afraid of knocking over a rack or of someone darting out in front of him.

She motioned for him to come across the gray carpet over to a corner where there was a display of kimonos. "Is this for your sister?"

He smiled and bowed his head.

"A friend?"

He nodded.

"Do you know her size?"

He looked puzzled. He pointed toward the lady.

"About my size?" She asked.

He nodded bashfully.

She smiled. "What color?"

He steered across to a black one.

"That's a nice one. Do you want it gift wrapped?"

He grinned and nodded.

"I'll be right back."

Betty would look great in that.

Megan's vacation.
Jerry's scare at four a.m.
This is real friendship.

Chapter 9

Sunday Evening: Jerry's computer and reading light were on. He was reading an electronic letter that Betty had sent him through an on-line service. He grinned.

The phone rang. He jumped. That startle reflex was still in good working condition. His left hand hit the rocker switch to the side of the keyboard turning on the speaker phone. "Hello."

"Jerry."

"Megan? You just left."

"I know. I just wanted to let you know that I had ground up some fruit for your helper, Cathy, for tomorrow."

"Thanks. That will save some time. But you don't have to worry about me for a whole week. That's one of the conditions of a vacation."

"I know. But, I thought I'd try to make it a little easier for the other aides."

"For a second, I thought you were worried about me."

"Me. Worried about you, not on your life. A week of freedom from the Old Man." Megan chuckled. "A whole week without you bugging me. My mind could use the rest. You have dear Cathy tomorrow morning."

"Can you make reservations at the nearest asylum?"

"Oh, Jerry, I thought you liked to listen to people's problems. Remember. You wanted to be a psychologist. Here's your chance!"

"Be quiet."

"Why, I'm not working now. I can say whatever I feel like. And while you're with Cathy tomorrow, I'll probably be at the beach."

"You just called to torment me."

"How did you guess?"

"I'm shrewd that way. Is Rick home?"

"He's working late. At least, I hope he is. Hey, I might have time to call Bob."

"Bob?"

"That guy I met at AA."

"I thought he was out of the picture."

"I just haven't said anything."

"You're a sneak."

"Not really. You haven't asked. You have my mom's number. I'll be there part of the time."

"Have a good time." He pushed the rocker switch hanging up the phone.

Monday Morning: Jerry awakened just before eight and remembered that Cathy would probably be there soon. She didn't have a key to his apartment. He kicked the blankets off and got into his chair. It was warm last night when Betty left so he just had a T-shirt on. He hoped that Betty had made it to work on time. The movie that they had rented was longer than they had expected. He couldn't remember a thing about the movie. It was nice just holding each other.

The hallway seemed to get longer each time he needed to unlock the front door in the morning. These young aides didn't know what they were asking from this old gentleman when they came so early. Three more pushes and he reached his front door. His hand couldn't grasp the knob the right way. This was one of the suspenseful aspects of having cerebral palsy, not knowing when your hands were going to work. He finally got the door unlocked.

He pushed himself back into his bedroom to wait. He started to put on his sweat pants and then heard the front door open. It was Cathy.

"Jerry, are you there? Oh, there you are. Goodness, I met this girl, Sally, on the bus who had a daughter with multiple scleroses and Sally didn't even know mouth-to-mouth. What kind of mother is that? But, I wonder if it's really her daughter."

Cathy was short and her skin seemed to have been filled up with Jell-O that shook when she moved. Her rounded face, topped with fine blond hair, was never in sync with the Jell-O. "Need help with your pants?"

"Please."

She bounced across the room and helped with Jerry's pants. He stood up by holding the bar near the toilet. "Fred in trailer forty-four has pink underwear hanging on the clothes line. The couple in forty-six think he is gay but Frank in fourteen said that we can't judge by underwear alone."

"Cathy."

"Yes?"

"What trailer?"

"I moved into a trailer court. Jim and I do our homework together."

"You moved in with Jim?"

"Don't be silly. Jim is in my nursing class."

"Oh. I would like toast and jelly with milk for breakfast."

"Can you believe Jim likes kids' cereal? I do too. My God, we have something in common. I'm so excited." She bounced out of the bedroom and down the hall. He assumed she was making his breakfast.

He wheeled over, picked up the stick for dialing the phone and dialed number four. "Delgado Independent Living Center."

"Sam, please."

Tammy recognized Jerry's voice. "Are you all right?"

"Yes, thanks."

"I typed up that last grant request you wrote. I hope it's approved. Barbara really needs a new chair."

"You never know how the people at the Medicare office are going to respond. You'd better retype it and have it ready to send again. This time make the last paragraph the second paragraph and take out her middle name."

"Good idea. Tricky too. I love it. Here's Sam."

"Sam here." Even those two words seemed labored, but perhaps knowing Sam was often on a respirator just made Jerry imagine it.

"Sam, it's me, Jerry. Can you handle that presentation alone?"

"Busy night with Betty?" He laughed.

"I have Cathy this morning."

"Where's Megan?"

"She needed a week off."

"She will be back Monday won't she? We have those stuffed shirts coming down."

"I told Megan about Monday. She promised to put me back together."

"Good. I can handle today. I really don't mind taking credit for your work."

"You're such a friend."

"Anytime, Jerry. Incidentally, enjoy all the Jim stories. I have another call." The phone went dead. Sure he has another call.

Jim stories? Jerry wondered what he was talking about. Jerry put down the stick and wheeled out of his bedroom, down the hall, and into the kitchen. There he found Cathy buttering a piece of toast, but instead of breaking it up for him, she took a bite. She was startled. "I didn't have time to eat before leaving home. I'll fix yours now. I hope you don't mind."

"It's okay." He decided to stay with Cathy and watch. He remembered when, Megan had bought him a whole loaf of bread, after she had eaten a slice of his one day. This was unlikely to ever happen with Cathy.

"Jim has a tattoo on his right shoulder. Just guess what it is? A little blue bird." She started making another piece of toast. "Can you believe that? It's so cute. I wonder if he has any other tattoos on other parts of his body?"

She brought the second piece of toast over and finally began feeding Jerry. "Don't men in jail have tattoos?" She continued. "He might be an undercover policeman and has that tattoo to act as part of the mob. That would be a shame."

The first bite she gave Jerry was too large and he choked. She slapped his back and he coughed up the piece of toast. At least he could have choked on something good like a steak, he thought. It just wasn't his day.

Still talking, Cathy said, "If Jim really is mixed up with the mob, maybe I should stay away. What do you think?"

Clearing his throat, he said, "You better be careful." He realized then just how long that morning was going to be. Jim stories. . .

Wednesday Evening: Jerry was sitting at the dining room table and Tom, an evening aide, came out of the bedroom. He was tall and was wearing green pants with an orange shirt opened half way down showing stringy chest hair. His mustache wasn't trimmed and hung down into his mouth. It had pieces of food hanging from the ends.

"Do you want to eat now?" Tom asked Jerry as he carried two glasses towards the kitchen. One with water in it and another glass with a little coffee in the bottom. Cathy had left these in the bedroom, so Jerry could get a drink while he was alone during the day.

"Yes. Soup."

"I have it on the stove. Are you going to tell Sam what a good job I'm doing?" He stumbled over the rubber border on the rug almost dropping the cups. "Sorry."

"Just relax. You'll do all right." Jerry sure had some things he wanted to tell Sam. Try out a new aide, sure! Sam probably interviewed this guy over the phone and sent him over here sight unseen. Tom spooned up some soup that had steam rising from it. "Too hot." Jerry said, pushing himself away from the spoonful of hot soup Tom was trying to feed him.

"Eat."

"TOO HOT."

"What?"

When Jerry started to say something else, Tom jammed the hot soup into Jerry's mouth. Jerry yelled and spit out the soup. "Idiot."

"Was that too hot?" Tom looked perplexed.

Jerry shouted, "I tried to tell you! Give me some

water."

"I don't like people who yell at me."

"I don't like hot soup jammed into my mouth. Couldn't you see the steam?"

"I can't see that well. See how thick my glasses are." His glasses were so dirty that it was a wonder he was able to see anything at all.

"Didn't you feel how hot the spoon was?"

"I have to catch a bus. I want to go watch a baseball game. Sam said you would pay me."

Jerry got the black bag from his electric wheelchair. "A ten dollar bill is in here."

Tom found the money and walked toward the door. "I just have five minutes to catch the bus."

"I didn't get my dinner."

"I might miss the first inning. Sorry, got to run." He rushed out the front door.

Jerry first put a straw into his mouth and then stuck the other end in the soup. He was only able to get a few sips. He was still hungry. He dialed number three on the phone, Rodney's number.

"Hello?"

"Rodney," Jerry said.

"Yes."

"Come over."

"Okay, be right there." Jerry unlocked the door. In a few minutes, Rodney bounded through the door. "What's up?"

"Would you fix me some chocolate milk please?"

"What do I get?"

"A piece of candy."

"A quarter."

"What?"

"I'm older than Craig. I'm twelve. You pay other people to do things for you. Why not me?"

"Okay."

"Great." Rodney rushed into the kitchen, made the chocolate milk, and set it on the table. Then Rodney grabbed the money bag and brought it over to Jerry to show him he had just taken a quarter. "I was wondering where I was going to get the twenty-five cents I needed for that poster." Right before he closed the door, he smiled. "Call anytime."

Early Friday Morning: Jerry suddenly jumped awake. Someone was breaking into his apartment. He was helpless. Mom never wanted him to be alone all night. He felt his heart race and adrenaline shoot throughout his body. It seemed like an hour waiting for something to happen. But what could he do? He couldn't get to the phone.

"Jerry."

He moved his mouth but no noise came. Megan! He tried twice before he could make any sound. "Yes." It was just Megan. His heart was still beating fast. Megan. Megan. Just breathe slowly. Breathe. Breathe.

She came back to his bedroom. "Jerry, are you all

right?" She rushed to his bed. "Jerry."

He struggled to talk. "You scared me."

She sat on the edge of the bed. "If anything ever happened to you. . ." She started to cry.

"Hey, I'm okay. You just have to take it easy on this old man."

She continued crying. "I'm so sorry. I should have called. I'm really sorry."

"No harm done."

"I left Rick."

"Gee. . . I thought it was serious. I was scared that you came by for your check."

She was crying and laughing at the same time. "Hold me."

He reached to hold her. She kicked off her shoes and laid down on top of the covers. She held him from behind, curling her body next to his. He felt her hair on the back of his neck. "Sorry about Rick." Jerry said softly.

"Don't be." Megan sobbed.

"He treated you badly."

"Is Betty good to you?"

"Very."

"Good."

Important events for the two.
Decisions to be carried through.
A big question to be asked.

Chapter 10

Jerry was finished in the bathroom so he just kicked off his gray sweats. He was glad he could work on the grant request for the handicapped center at home and didn't have to get dressed up. This was the one part of writing grants that he appreciated. Being the guy behind the scenes did have its advantages.

He threw the sweats into the dirty clothes basket and climbed back over into his wheelchair. Unlocking one side of the chair, he remembered how furious Betty had been with him when she discovered that he didn't lock his wheelchair before transferring to it. Before she would leave one night, he had to promise her he would always lock his chair.

He wheeled out of the bathroom across to his bedroom and opened a drawer to grab a clean pair of underwear. First, he put his right leg in and then the left, pulling the underwear up past his knees. Next, he wheeled across to his bed, locked both wheels, grabbed the bar, and swung himself onto the bed. Then he stretched out on his back.

He rolled onto his left side and pulled his underwear up as far as he could with his right hand. Then he rolled onto his right side pulling the underwear up with his left hand. He repeated this a number of times, pulling the underwear up a little bit each time he rolled from side to side. He did this until the underwear was in the right position. He was convinced that putting on his underwear this way was of great aerobic value to him.

He turned over and looked at Betty's picture and thought how remarkable she was. She looked beyond his physical appearance and heard over his distorted speech.

Suddenly, the front door opened and slammed. "This man wants me to hoof it over here twice in one day." Megan trooped into the bedroom. "What is this? Lying down?"

"I just changed my underwear," Jerry said.

"Well good. Less work for me." She strolled over to the bed and helped him sit up. "Nancy, my new roommate, told me that you called. Didn't you think I would remember you wanted me to come back?"

"I just wanted to make sure. You have a lot on your mind lately. How did Rick take the news?"

She helped Jerry into his chair. "Oh, he blamed me for everything."

"What did you expect? What about Bob?"

"Bob is so sweet. He brought a rose for me to the last AA meeting, when he heard how Rick was treating me." She wet a cloth and washed off Jerry's chest.

He raised both arms, so Megan could wash his underarms. "Tell me about Bob."

She rinsed the soap out of the cloth and wiped his body down once more. "Oh, Bob is just a friend. He is just someone to talk with. After that time with Rick, I need to be alone for a while."

"I know what you mean. After Ann left, I didn't want to be with anyone for a good year. I'm proud of how you handled this Rick thing."

"Thanks, Rick thought everyone but he had a problem. I'm glad that's over."

He moved toward his closet. "I would like to wear my black suit."

She reached for the suit. "Do you have to go to a special function for The Center?"

"No. I handed in my notice, and after these two grant requests, I'm out of there. I'm Long Beach bound. My old position opened up and the director of Handicapped Services called me personally."

"That's great. But, why the suit tonight?" She started to help him put on his pants.

He held onto the bar next to the bed so she could pull them up. "I have important matters to attend to involving one Betty."

Megan smiled. "You aren't going to pop the big question?"

"I'm not getting dressed up just to go to the hamburger joint."

"You didn't tell me things had gotten that serious." She started to help him put on his shirt.

"As I said, you've been busy with your business. And I have had pressing business of my own."

"Jerry, this is exciting." She buttoned his shirt.

"If this is good, why do I feel sick to my stomach?"

"That's normal."

"What if she says no?"

"What if she says yes?"

"I need an aspirin."

Megan sat down on the bed. "Jerry, you made a life outside the institution. You held down two jobs after people told you that you couldn't. And now you're worried about this?"

"But, this is different."

"Well, all I can say is, Betty is a lucky woman."

"You really think so?"

"Sometimes, you're hopeless." Megan laughed, as she pulled down the bed covers as part of her evening duties. "I'm getting away from this crazy man." Megan hugged him. "You're going to be just fine." With that, she said good-bye and left him with a wave.

It seemed very quiet. The sounds of the kids playing just outside seemed far away. Their playing usually drove him nuts.

He studied his image in the mirror. There sat a man with graying black hair and a neatly trimmed beard. He had on a black jacket with silvery threads running through it, a thin black tie, and a maroon shirt. The little finger on his left hand had a red mark from moving his hand back and forth across the plastic template that covered his computer keyboard.

He felt an internal peace with none of the anger or hatred of the past. This was Betty's man.

The doorbell rang. "Coming." Jerry pushed his chair out of his bedroom and started down the hall.

A happy man.

This time was bound to come.
How to tell Jerry.
With each success, comes some pain.

Chapter 11

The first light of Wednesday morning peeked above the mustard-yellow colored Winchell's Donut sign. Megan pulled open the glass door and scrambled into the small shop where Ken was working. It had just two benches and four rounded stools anchored to a table. She was wearing nursing uniform pants with a pale orange smock.

Behind the glass case, cinnamon twists, glazed, and jelly doughnuts lay on thin waxed paper. The aroma of the pastries filled the room. Megan dropped the bags, containing her change of clothes and schoolbooks, on the nearest table. "Hi, Ken. I'll tell you, I'm beat. I just pulled an all-nighter at that rest home down the street."

"You have to make extra money anywhere you can these days," Ken responded.

"May I have two glazed, one jelly doughnut, and one large black coffee?"

"Sure thing. The jelly one's for Jerry?" Ken reached through the back of the case and started picking up each doughnut separately with waxed paper.

"Yeah." A muddy fog encased her mind. She reached across the case and took the doughnuts from Ken and set them on the table before walking back to pay him.

"Thanks." Ken said, taking the money.

"Sure." She said, as he turned around to go to the back room to start rolling out some more dough. She stepped back and squeezed herself between the stool and the table. She took a sip of the coffee and opened her small purse. She then pulled out the letter and read it again.

Dear Megan Williams,

After carefully reviewing your application, we are happy to inform you that you have been accepted into The Anaheim Graduate School in The Child Development Department.

Classes begin August 15. Your advisor will be Ms. Vicki Walken.

We look forward to hearing from you at your earliest convenience.

Sincerely,

Joe Foster
Director of Graduate Studies

She laid down the letter. It had been a whole year since she had applied for that program. In one month, she would be finished with her classes here and then on to a new school in a new town. She got some change out and started to walk over to call her mom on the pay phone, but changed her mind. Mom wouldn't care if she went to school or not. So she took a bite of the donut.

Megan couldn't wait to tell Jerry. As she started to take another bite, the reality of actually leaving Jerry sank in. How could she leave him? How could they find someone to help on such short notice? He started his new job next week. He needed her, or someone, to care for him, or he wouldn't be able to keep that job for long.

She remembered several years ago when she hadn't been able to work for Jerry for about six months and had come by for a visit. His hair looked as if it hadn't been combed in days. His clothes appeared as if they just had been thrown on him. Part of the reason, that she had accepted the job at the church, was that it would allow her to work for Jerry at the same time. She took another bite of her doughnut, while she tried to think of a friend who could take her place. Most people wanted a full-time job, but Jerry only needed help for a few hours in the morning and then again in the late afternoon.

How was she going to tell Jerry? She slowly cleaned up the table, gathered up her belongings, and walked out the door. "See you later, Ken."

"So long, Megan." The sun was up now, but it was overcast.

Just a block away, Jerry, waiting for Megan, had gotten out of bed and partly dressed himself. He wheeled into the living room and pulled the rope cord that opened the window curtain. He heard Brooks hurrying down the stairs on his way to junior high school. Soon, other kids scrambled past on their way to school. He had known most of them since they were babies.

Victoria hurried past, probably on her way to college. She had come over one night to give him his medicine.

He was getting cold, sitting there in just a T-shirt. He pushed his chair backward down the hall to the heater thermostat switch. It had been installed low enough for him to reach. He slid the control upward, so the heater would turn on. He went back down the hall and returned to the window.

He looked at the apartment across from his and saw Anna. She had never been the same after her husband had killed himself. Anna had always helped Jerry with his seat belt. He wished he could help her in some way, but her mental state was so unstable that it wasn't safe for Jerry to even visit her now. All that he could do was to keep her in his prayers.

Then Marci rushed past. She had lived there the longest of any tenant and she was always working on a secret plan to move somewhere else. This "secret plan," at least, provided a reason for her to get up each day.

A few minutes after eight, he suddenly became nervous. What if Megan wasn't coming? What could he do? Most of his neighbors had gone to work and all the kids had left for school by now. He could ask Anna to help, but if she hadn't taken her medication, she would come over partly dressed and merely stand there in the doorway and rock back and forth on her heels. Betty had left some candy out on the table but he had devoured that shortly after she had left.

He knew there was milk in the refrigerator, but he couldn't get it out without dropping it. He could knock some food on the floor and get down and pick it up with his mouth but he would be quickly joined by the building's cockroaches.

He stared out the window. What would he do, if Megan had been hurt in a car accident? What if Rick found out where her new place was, broke in, and beat her up? She might be in the hospital or alone and hurt somewhere.

In a few seconds, Megan strolled past and waved. She unlocked the front door. "Up early?"

Jerry's heart beat returned to normal and he relaxed. Megan was there. "Yes, I just couldn't sleep any more. What's with the uniform?"

"I worked all night at The Becker Rest Home. Nancy moved without paying her part of the rent, so I needed the money." She threw her bags on the couch.

"You really haven't had much luck with roommates. Need an advance?"

Megan tramped across the room and dropped into a chair. "Jerry, please." She looked troubled.

He wheeled over and folded both arms on the table top. "Trouble with Bob?"

"No. He is so good to me."

"Mom up to her old tricks?"

"I haven't heard from her in weeks."

"Ants in your underwear?"

She laughed. "I have something to tell you and don't know how." She paused. "Remember some time back I sent in an application for graduate school?"

"Yeah, I think so."

"You helped me with that letter?"

"Yeah."

"I received a reply. I was accepted. I start in six weeks."

He went over and hugged her. "I'm so proud of you. You did it. You did it."

He was grabbing her so hard that he was about to pull her off the chair. "Jerry, wait. Wait. There's more."

He relaxed his hold. "They bought you a new car?"

She climbed back on the kitchen chair. "One of your hugs is going to kill me someday." She hesitated before telling him. "Jerry, the school is about a hundred miles away."

"Good. New town. New people. Best thing for you."

"I won't be able to work for you, after this month."

"Bad. Bad town. You have enough friends right here. It would be the worst thing for you."

"Jerry, I've been going crazy ever since I got this letter. I don't want to leave you."

He sat still. He didn't want to cry in front of her. The nightmare would begin again of finding someone to help him. "You have been good to me."

"You have been good to me too." They reached across and held each other.

He finally pulled away and wiped the tears from his face. "I'll call Sam. He might know of someone."

"I thought The Center wasn't a good place to find help anymore."

"Well, Sam gave me his home phone number. We go back to way before we worked at The Center." Jerry just had to say something, to make her feel better. Sam had enough trouble finding helpers for himself and others who called him.

"Is there any chance that Betty could help out, if we can't find someone by the time I have to leave?" She brushed her hair away from her damp face.

"Betty and I decided, last week, not to see each other as often as before."

"Oh, Jerry, I'm sorry to hear that. From what you told me, you were good for one another."

"Don't count this old horse out yet. We are still going to see each other. I'm cooking up some juicy e-mail."

"Betty doesn't have a chance." Megan smiled. "I brought a jelly doughnut."

"What, a last meal for a condemned man?"

"Jerry!"

"Okay. No more jokes." The jelly doughnut seemed tasteless. He pondered what it would be like without Megan. He could find someone to care for his needs, but he had watched Megan turn from a teenager into a beautiful young woman. She was like his daughter.

"Want to just get dressed now? I can come back tonight to give you your shower."

He nodded. Who would he have to really talk to now? Whom could he call, if he got sick late at night? Who would make him laugh, if he used four letter words when he thought he was alone?

"I'll see you about five. Are you all right?" Megan said, as she walked down the hall.

"Sure." He lied.

"Get some sleep." He heard the front door close and the lock turn. He spoke softly. "I love you, Megan."

He is relieved to see his care provider, even if she is late.

Reflections.
The search begins.
Life goes on.

Chapter 12

Monday, 9:00 a.m. Jerry picked up his typing stick and dialed his phone.

"Good morning, Delgado Independent Living Center. How can I help you?" It was Tammy on the telephone.

"If you weren't married, you could help me in many ways."

"Oh, Jerry," Tammy answered and then whispering into the mouthpiece, she said, "There are a lot of stuffed shirts here now. It hasn't been as much fun around here, since you left."

"Thanks, Tammy. Is Sam busy?"

"I'll see. Call me at home when you get a chance."

"I sure will." He leaned back in his chair and waited for Sam. He missed working at The Center, the way it was back in the old days, when it had been small enough that everyone got to know everyone else. Each person who had called The Center was made to feel important. Now each caller was merely asked what department they wanted. If it was someone new calling, he or she was sent a form to fill out before they could talk to anyone. Jerry just couldn't work in that kind of system.

A few seconds passed and then Sam came on the

phone. "Hello, this is Sam. How can I help you?"

"Oh, Sam, you sound so professional."

"Jerry! Why didn't you tell me it was you before I went through my whole speech?"

"I just wanted to make sure you're doing your job the proper way." Jerry chuckled, knowing how Sam loathed the idea of doing his job by set guidelines.

"Very funny! I have three calls to return and this progress report needs to be done by six."

"So, not much has changed, in the two weeks I have been gone."

"No. The only thing different is, it was decided not to hire someone to take your place, and I have to handle two jobs now."

"You had enough to handle with your own job."

"Haven't you heard? I'm Super Handicapped Man." His frustration could be felt, even over the phone. "Enough about me. When do you start your new job? What's up?"

"I start next week. The reason I called is, Megan has to move and can only work for two more weeks."

"How can you start a new job and train an aide at the same time? "

"Super Handicapped Man number two?"

"Wait a second." Jerry heard Sam's electric wheelchair wheeling across his office, the door being pushed shut, and his chair coming back to the phone. "You know, your name isn't very popular around here, since you quit."

"That was what I figured. I don't want to cause you any trouble."

"Don't worry about that. Have you started calling around?"

"You are my first call."

"There is Patti, but she is already working with three people. I'll let you know, if someone else looks promising."

"How can Patti manage that? The last time I talked with her she was going to school." Once, Patti became a little too friendly, while giving Jerry a shower, and after that he never felt comfortable with her. He truly didn't want Patti as his aide, but it might come to that. However, if Betty ever wanted to get that friendly, he wouldn't have any problem. In fact, he'd be happy to give Betty a shower.

"Jerry, are you still there?" Sam asked.

Jerry sat straight up in his chair. "Yeah . . . uh, I was just trying to think what my next move should be."

"I heard yesterday, The State is trying to cut the funds for care providers again."

"If the funds are cut any more, it would become almost impossible to find anyone to do this type of work. I already use a hundred dollars of my own money, which is meant for living expenses, to pay people to help me. At this rate, I won't have enough money to buy the food for aides to feed me."

"I know what you mean. If mom hadn't left money in her Will, especially to be spent on my care, I couldn't afford someone to be with me around the clock like I need. I would have to go into a rest home."

Jerry responded. "I did my time in a rest home. I would rather die than go back to one of those places."

"Yeah, and to think paying for care providers to come to your home costs the state one third of the price of institutionalizing you. All this makes my stomach hurt," Sam added.

Jerry remarked, "I didn't think you had any feeling below your chest."

"See what I mean? I have to take another call. Let me know what happens." The line went dead.

Monday, 2:30 p.m. Jerry pulled out a file and tried to put it on the counter next to his computer keyboard but some of the papers fell out. A few of the papers landed on the counter and a couple on the floor. They were just scraps of paper with the names and phone numbers of people who were once his aides. There were also numbers for people who had come to interviews and then didn't come back on the day they were scheduled to start work. Some of these scraps just had names without numbers and others had numbers without names. Jerry thought he would remember what name went to what number but his long-term memory didn't work as well as his computer memory.

He tried to push most of the strips of paper to the back

of the counter, but more of them fell on the floor in the process. He took a disgusted breath and then reached under the counter and grabbed the waste paper basket. He could easily manage it with its two large square handles.

He dumped all the trash from the trash basket on his bed and then he laid the basket on the floor. With his foot, he kicked each scrap of paper into the wastebasket. He once would have picked up each strip one-by-one. But, he had recently discovered the added paunch around his middle made this activity extremely uncomfortable. But, rather than admit that perhaps eating less candy at bedtime would improve his ability to do physical activity. He preferred to think of using the basket as a more efficient way to perform this task.

After he had pushed all the scraps of paper into the waste basket, he dumped them on the counter. Then he threw the trash on the bed back into the basket and shoved the basket under the counter.

He picked up one of the scraps and it had the name Jack and a phone number. Jack had worked a few weekends and he hadn't been too bad. Another paper had April written on it. She was one of the good ones. She was always on time, even when she had to bring her six-year-old son. Jerry put this note aside. April worked in a bank now, but she might be available for weekends.

Jerry glanced at his watch. It was almost three o'clock. Megan would be there soon with a lady to interview for the aide position. He ripped off the computer printout of questions he usually asked new aides. Just as he reached the living room, Megan walked in with an older lady.

"This is Jerry," Megan said.

"Hello, Jerry, my name is May." She was tall with brown pants that were well worn and her white tennis shoes had almost turned black. She had a brown and white sweater which was pulled tightly around her extended stomach, which made Jerry wonder if she had a drinking problem. Her hair was piled up on her head like that of an old schoolmarm and her skin had the milky white tone of someone who might have been living in a cave the last ten or twenty years.

"Would you like to sit down?" Jerry asked her.

Megan explained. "Jerry said, 'Would you like to sit down?'."

May replied, "Thank you." May sat down on the couch but she couldn't get comfortable.

Megan sat in a chair next to the window. Jerry waited a minute and then wheeled over to where May was sitting. "Have you taken care of a handicapped person before?"

Megan again repeated what Jerry had just said.

"No, but I'm willing to learn," May replied.

"Sometimes, it's easier to work with someone who doesn't have any experience."

Megan again repeated what Jerry had just said and added that she too hadn't had any experience when she started.

Jerry wheeled closer and handed May the computer printout. "This is a general outline of the care I need."

May glanced through the papers. "Gee, I think I would get scared, if he got something stuck in his throat."

Megan said. "That doesn't happen very often."

May stood up and walked toward the door. "Sorry, I was just looking for a house cleaning job." May left. Jerry and Megan stared at each other.

Tuesday, 2:00 p.m. Jerry was searching through the scraps of notes spread out on his computer counter. He found one with the name Doug and immediately tore up this note and threw it away. Nobody knew that Doug had serious mental problems. It took Jerry five years to get that guy out of his life.

The doorbell rang and Jerry remembered right then that Dave, the wheelchair repair man, had called and scheduled an appointment. Jerry propelled his chair backwards down the hall and into the living room.

When Jerry opened his front door, Dave, a husky man, stood before him wearing a T-shirt that had a green skull, with bright red eyes, printed on the front. His hair was kinky and didn't cover as much of his forehead as it once had. In his right hand was a tool box and in his left he had a cardboard box bulging with wheels.

"Avon calling," said Dave, with a straight face.

"Dave, come in." Jerry moved back so Dave could get past. "Did you bring the whole store?"

"Did I bring. . . Sorry, I didn't understand that one. I haven't been around you in a while. No speak the Jerry talk." Jerry started to reach for his spell board and Dave said. "No, not the cursed spell board. We have known each other for over eight years. Don't humiliate me by using the spell board."

Jerry repeated himself.

This time, Dave got it. "No. I just brought half of the store." After setting everything down, he walked over and shook Jerry's hand. "How is my old friend?"

"I'm hanging in there."

"It was good to get your FAX. The people in the office got a big kick out of you calling me 'The King of Wheelchair Repair.' May I get a glass of water? The gate was locked and I had to hike half a block with all my tools. Can I get you anything?"

"Help yourself. I'm okay" Jerry pointed to where the glasses were. "I would have met you by the gate. . ."

Dave fixed himself some ice water. "I know, but I had no idea how long my last appointment was going to be." He sipped the water and strolled over and sat down on the arm of the couch. "This guy had been in bed for six months and his family just fed him once a day. It looked and smelled like he hadn't ever had a bath."

"Can't you report that to someone?"

"It would just be my word against theirs. Besides, he has cancer and will probably die in six months to a year. I moved his bed over to the window so he could look out."

He sipped his water. "So you need new front tires?" He stood up and walked over to Jerry's electric wheelchair.

"I think the left wheel is bent." Jerry said, following Dave. "I hope it isn't too bad."

"Most people just take their chairs from room to room but you drive yours like a truck."

"Can I help it if the store is two blocks away?"

"Most people, with your degree of disability, ask their aides to do the shopping."

"Mom and dad wanted me to be as independent as possible."

"I'm glad they did, but I don't think they meant for you to travel all across the county in a wheelchair."

"Well, you're the one who convinced the people at Medicare to purchase an electric wheelchair for me."

"That was three wheelchairs ago."

"It wasn't my fault the last two didn't hold up to my lifestyle."

Dave laughed. "I just wanted to give you more independence. I didn't know I was creating Evil Kinevil in a wheelchair. I still have nightmares of you driving your chair across that freeway overpass in the traffic lane."

"What else could I do? There wasn't any ramp to the sidewalk. Can I help it if, the more I saw of the outside world, the more I wanted to see?"

"I guess not." Dave walked across and bent down to take a closer look at the electric wheelchair. "Jerry, man, you wore these tires down almost to the rims."

"Did I bend the rims?" Jerry anxiously moved forward. If the rims were bent, the chair might have to be taken to the shop and he would be without it for several days.

He would not only then be unable to do his own shopping but he would also be unable to go visit friends around the neighborhood. And, he couldn't take rides in the park when he needed to just get away to think. He would not have any way to visit that homeless young black man who always said, "Hi," and asked how he was doing. Jerry couldn't remember his name but they needed to talk to each other once in a while just to touch another human being. And to connect so the problems of living didn't seem so overwhelming.

"No, Jerry, the rims are okay. I can fix it right here." Dave pulled the new tires out of the box. Jerry watched Dave's large hands and fingers nimbly undo bolts and take off wheels. Jerry never was envious of someone like Dave, who could use his hands. He merely appreciated their ability. "There you go. Good for another five hundred miles . . . well in your case, maybe two hundred." He packed up his tools and threw away the old tires. "May I wash my hands in the kitchen?"

"Sure. There is some liquid soap on the sink. Off for home now?"

"Not yet. There is a two-year old boy thirty miles away who I need to measure for a new wheelchair."

"Aren't kids hard for you to work with knowing what battles they have ahead?"

"I don't think about it. It's just a job."

"That doesn't have anything to do with your stomach problems?"

"Nothing gets by you, does it?"

"Not much."

"Call me if you have any more problems. Take care my friend."

"You too."

Wednesday, 1:00 p.m. Jerry looked at the clock on the wall just to the right of his computer. It was almost time to meet someone named Sally at the back gate. She had answered an ad Jerry put in a weekly paper and was coming for an interview. He didn't have any idea who she was but he had to try something.

He usually liked to have Megan or someone with him when a new person first came. But, Megan had something else to do and couldn't come over when Sally could come.

He turned off his computer and pulled off his reading glasses. Just before he left his bedroom, he wheeled over to his sink and shoved two bottles of medication into a drawer. The same pills he needed to help his muscles relax also could make other people high. He hated to be so suspicious of people, but living alone all these years he had learned not to be too trusting.

He backed his chair out of the bedroom and pulled his

door almost closed. There wasn't any reason, to advertise all the computer equipment he had, before getting a feel for someone. He wheeled down the hall into the living room. He laid the papers for the interview on one end of the couch, picked up his money purse, and put it out of sight.

He wheeled over to the front door, opened it, turned his chair around, grabbed the brown cord, and backed down the wooden ramp. He didn't lock his door this time, because he could see his apartment from the gate. He pushed his chair backwards on the sidewalk. All the kids said, "Hi Jerry," when he passed. He returned the greetings.

He gave one final glance to his apartment as he approached the gate. The gate was locked, which didn't stop an approaching teenager from climbing over. "Hi Jerry," the teen said, after climbing over the gate and walking off.

Jerry tried to unlock the gate but couldn't. This was partly because it had a special covering to keep people from reaching over the gate to open it. The gate seemed to make up in inconvenience what it lacked in security.

A neighbor approached the gate from the outside and tried to open it with his key, but someone had stuffed bubble gum into the lock again. Frustrated, the neighbor went around to the driveway gate to wait for somebody to drive through so he could walk in behind the car.

Every time Jerry hired a new aide, he had to make a

new gate key, because past aides didn't return their keys. All this annoyance was for a gate that didn't work most of the time anyway, because kids put gum in the lock.

Another neighbor, who was leaving, walked past Jerry and opened the gate. She asked if Jerry wanted out. He shook his head but quickly put his left foot out to keep the gate from closing. Right then about ten school kids came through the gate and each one said, "Thank you, Jerry," as they squeezed between Jerry and the gate. Jerry was glad he worked on a computer rather than as a doorman, although the tips would be nice.

Sally had said that she would be driving a gray car. A green car passed. A light blue car, which might have been gray, slowed down. He thought it might be the one but then it sped past. He looked at his watch and he had been sitting there a good fifteen minutes. A yellow car and a red car passed.

Finally, after a half hour had passed, he let the gate bang shut and pushed his chair backward to his apartment. He didn't want to play doorman any longer. When he got back into his bedroom, there was a message on his answering machine: "This is Sally. I have found another position. Thank you."

An hour wasted. He set his medication back in its place and put his money bag back into his electric wheelchair. He threw the papers for the interview across the room.

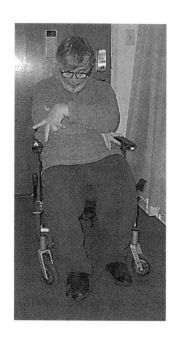

Thursday, 2:00 p.m. Megan answered Jerry's front door and there stood a guy wearing a white T-shirt. It was stretched across his belly so tight that it seemed it was about to rip. He had an untrimmed beard and one tennis shoe wasn't tied. "Hello, my name is John. I came for an interview." Jerry wondered how this guy could care for anyone else when he plainly was unable to care for himself.

"This is Jerry," Megan said. Jerry put out his hand, but John didn't take it.

"Would you like to sit down?" Megan asked John.

"Thanks. So, do you live here?"

"No. This is Jerry's apartment."

Jerry asked, "Where do you live?" Megan repeated what Jerry said.

"I'm living with friends right now. So, do you like to play pool?" He asked, eyeing Megan.

Jerry spoke so only Megan could understand him. "He wants you. Aren't you excited?"

She punched Jerry in the side. "John, have you taken care of a handicapped person before?"

"Yes, for about six months. It didn't work out. He was too demanding. That guy wanted to have breakfast at exactly the same time each day."

Jerry asked, "Do you have a phone?" Megan repeated Jerry's words.

"No. My friend does and I check with him about once a week."

Jerry said, "I have a few more interviews. Leave your friend's phone number and I'll get back to you."

After John left, Megan said, "I didn't think you had any other interviews."

"I'll find some."

Friday, 1:00 p.m. Jerry opened the front door and there stood a lady. She was about five feet tall, had long dark hair, and was wearing gray jeans and a blue flowered blouse. "Hi," she said, grinning, "my name is Cindy. I called earlier about an interview."

"Come in." Jerry moved his chair back and gestured for her to enter.

"You want me to come in?"

Jerry smiled and nodded. "Have a seat." He gestured toward the couch.

"You said 'Have a seat'?" Jerry smiled and nodded. "It may take me awhile to get used to the way you speak," she said.

"Don't worry about it."

"I got that one. Do you live here by yourself?" She sat down.

"Yes." He usually didn't let people know right away that he lived alone but Cindy seemed harmless. However, with his luck, she might be wanted in six states for armed robbery.

"I have worked for many handicapped people but none of them lived alone."

He rushed over and locked the front door. There is a God. Someone had answered his ad who was intelligent. "I like living alone."

"I'm sorry. I didn't get that." He pulled out his letter board and spelled out what he had said.

"I live alone with my son," she said. "He's eight years old."

Good. Good. She was stable and responsible. Jerry pointed to the papers on one end of the couch. "This will explain the type of help I need."

"Okay" She picked up the papers and started reading them but then cautiously laid the papers down making sure the papers were right back where they had been. "I don't think I can do this job."

He spelled out. "Why?"

"I have always worked for women. I could never help

a man in the bathroom. I'm sorry." She got up, walked toward the door, opened it, and hurried out.

He sat there with his mouth open. What happened?

Saturday evening: Jerry was lying on his bed. There were only two weeks to go before Megan left for college. He had lost count of how many interviews he had conducted. His computer desk was covered with scraps of paper that had names and phone numbers of people, who said that they were coming to be interviewed, but never showed up. Some called to say that they had found another job or they didn't feel this job was meant for them. Most did not even call. He wasn't sure now, how many times he had pushed his chair all the way out to the gate for nothing.

He turned over. He would call the college tomorrow. Surely, there must be one student who needs a job. Jerry was almost asleep when the doorbell rang. What? Had he forgotten that he had scheduled an interview? He climbed out of bed and got into his chair. Maybe this would be the right person for the job. He rushed down the hall and raced into the living room. He glanced at the couch. The papers for an interview were in their place.

He smiled and opened the door. It was Rodney. "Rodney!"

"Doesn't your computer have an on-line information service?"

Hesitating, Jerry said, "Yes."

"I have geography homework. I need to write a report

on France. I thought it would be neat to look up France on your computer."

"But, Rodney I'm tired."

"Please."

"Oh, okay."

"You're a pal." Rodney stepped around Jerry's chair and marched back to the room with the computer. Jerry closed the door. Rodney came back and pushed Jerry into the computer room.

"I need your password." Rodney moved all Jerry's papers into a neat pile. "I'll put them back right where they were." He searched around for a pencil. He found one and before he removed the special template from the top of the keyboard, he carefully made four small marks around the outside of it marking its position. "That way I can put the template back in the right place so you will be able to type. Also, Mom won't kill me because you have to call her late at night to put the template in the right place. Now, what is your password?"

"Forgot."

"What?"

"Forgot."

"You forgot your own password. Nobody forgets their password."

"No."

"Then, what is it?"

"Forgot."

"You just said you didn't forget it."

"I didn't."

"Jerry, you're driving me nuts. What is your stupid password?"

"I told you three times."

"You just said forgot."

"Right."

"Forgot is your password." Rodney started typing. "Why in the world did you pick forgot?"

"I didn't want to forget it."

"Jerry, you're insane." He typed on the computer. "This stuff will make a great report. Hey, why are so many people coming to see you this week?"

"Megan is moving away and can't help me any longer. I'm looking for someone else to help me."

"Gee, if we weren't moving, I could take care of you."

"I didn't know you were moving."

"Dad found a house near the high school." Rodney printed the material he needed, turned off the computer, replaced the template, and put Jerry's papers back where he had found them. Thanking Jerry, he waved good-bye and left.

First, Megan was leaving. Now, Craig and Rodney. Jerry laid down again and tried to go to sleep.

Two phone calls.
And, two new beginnings.
Tomorrow at eight.

Chapter 13

Jerry backed his chair down the wheelchair ramp that had a blue spot of paint from the last time they had painted the outside of the apartments. This spot reminded him that he had been there another two years. They only painted the outside of these apartments every two years.

He looked down into the red bag on the side of his chair and saw the notes that he had printed up and Megan had put there the night before. This was a fine how-do-you-do. He had to go out looking for an aide like a panhandler.

All the phone calls and interviews had been an exercise in futility. But, fool that he was, he had done this routine each time he needed an aide. He always thought well of the human race and that all people had good and honest hearts. He had been frequently disappointed on this point, but he still believed all humans were basically good. Some kind person out there would just love to become his aide. At times, he admitted, nobody loved cleaning him after he used the bathroom, but other than that, being his aide was the greatest job to come along. But, where were these good-hearted souls when he needed an aide?

Sam had not called him back for days. Sam probably was busy doing reports that were due at the end of the month. The paperwork at The Center went on, even when they couldn't help somebody find an aide. Jerry didn't want to become bitter, like other clients at The Center, but he knew how they worked over there and it was becoming more impersonal.

Oh well, Jerry did not have to deal with that part of the system. He never was cut out for it. He had to concentrate on finding an aide. His new job at Long Beach was only one week away. It would be nice to get out again around people who were active. The job at Long Beach was more his style.

Once again, he looked down at the bag and made sure he was able to pull out one note at a time.

The notes read:
Disabled man needs help two times a day
from 8 a.m. to 11 a.m. and from 4 p.m. to 6 p.m.
Needs help with showering, dressing, cooking,
eating, and other personal care. Pays $5.50 an
hour. Call Jerry at 555-1212.

He put his hand on the joystick and made his chair go down the walkway past Rodney and Craig's apartment. He would miss Rodney and Craig. They had been like sons to him. He went by Anna's apartment. The visiting nurse came out of it and walked by Jerry. The nurse told

Jerry that Anna was doing much better. Jerry guided his chair down the walkway, to the right, and out into the alley.

He passed by a couple and the lady kissed her husband good-bye. Jerry wished he had kissed Betty good-bye the last time he saw her. He felt an emptiness inside, realizing just how long it had been since he had seen her.

He had to find an aide. Megan had to move away in about a week. He drove his chair through the gate and out on Hunt Street. A woman walked toward Jerry. She looked kind and clean. Jerry reached down for a note and pulled out one but the lady just walked on by. He put the note back and guided his chair down to the corner.

While Jerry was waiting for the light to change, a lady walked by, but he didn't reach for a note. She looked down and out and probably wasn't able to care for herself much less for another person.

Jerry's first stop was the grocery store. Just inside the door there was a bulletin board with yellow three-by-five cards. This was where people put up notices about selling cars or other things. John, a box boy, walked toward Jerry. "Hey, big guy, need to do some shopping? All the pretty girls are on break so you're stuck with me."

Jerry pulled out one of his notes and handed it to him. "Please put this up there."

John took the note. "Oh, no, not again. Another helper split on you." He took the note and folded it so it would fit neatly on the board. "There, is that all right?"

Jerry nodded. "Thanks."

"No problem. Have any shopping?"

"Not now."

"Jerry, you sly dog. You will probably come back later when Erica is working. I saw you eyeing her."

Jerry grinned. "Maybe so."

"It's getting busy. I have to run. Good luck in finding someone." He hurried back to the check stands and started bagging groceries.

Jerry looked at his note on the board. He knew he never got any responses from this board. A box boy made more than Jerry could pay an aide. But, he needed to try everything.

He had planned to go to another grocery store, but instead, guided his chair to the bar where he had once spent many nights. The paint, on the bottom of the doorframe, still had marks from where his wheelchair had scraped it while entering and leaving the bar.

In a few days, Megan would walk out of his life. Whom could he really talk and laugh with from now on? Megan wasn't his wife or even his girlfriend, but the loss was still the same. He stared at the bar door. The sickening smell of beer and stale cigarette smoke made his stomach turn. The bar was not the answer. He guided his chair down the street. There had to be a better way.

He didn't feel like handing out any more notes right then. He didn't want to go back to his apartment either. It just reminded him of the problem of finding someone to take Megan's place. Instead, he decided to go to Jack-in-the-Box for a coke.

He guided his chair down the street and turned the corner. He headed toward the door of Jack-in-the-Box. Some people, who were leaving, held the door for him so he sped inside. He glanced around and the fellow who usually helped him wasn't there. He pulled out his letter board for the clerk and spelled out "I w-o-u-l-d l-i-k-e a c-o-k-e."

"One dollar, please." The young boy said.

Jerry put his moneybag on the counter and the boy pulled out a dollar. Then, Jerry guided his chair over to a table. The two high school boys behind the counter had the great debate over what to do next. Finally, one of them brought Jerry's coke over and set it on the table.

Jerry started to take a sip and realized he had not asked to have the top left off. This meant the straw came out through a hole in the middle of the lid. This made it easier for him to tip over the cup accidentally. Without the lid, the straw was free to move around in the cup and not tip it over.

So, now, every time he put his mouth on the straw, the cup would move a little and threaten to tip over. This game was called, "How Much of The Coke Would He Get Before The Cup Falls Over?"

He took the first sip and the cup just moved a little. He eyeballed the space between the cup and the edge of the table. If his calculations were right, he could get three more sips before the cup would fall off the table. He could have asked someone behind the counter to take off the top but he was in a sporting mood.

He was about to take his second sip when he spotted a heavyset woman in the corner booth eating a jumbo hamburger. She had long brown hair down past her waist. After Jerry took another sip the woman asked, "Would you like me to hold the cup?"

"Yes." Jerry said. The lady had a puzzled expression so he wheeled over to the booth and pulled out his letter board and spelled what he had just said.

The lady smiled, "My name is Margie. What is yours?"

"Jerry," he said.

"Larry?" she asked.

"Jerry," he repeated.

"Harry?"

Jerry spelled out his name.

"That letter board is a great idea. Do you want me to bring your drink over here?" she asked.

He nodded, "Yes." She brought his drink over to her table. He took a sip. The cup moved towards the table edge.

She reached over and moved Jerry's drink away from the edge of the table. "Do you live around here?"

He nodded again and said, "Yes."

"I usually don't come to this part of town but I had a

job interview. I have carpal tunnel syndrome so I can't do assembly work anymore. But, it seemed like they were looking for a girl who wore a short skirt and giggled each time the boss walked past, instead of a receptionist. I stopped to eat before heading home. I eat a lot when I'm frustrated."

He imagined himself in a cartoon with a flashing light saying "SOMEONE WHO NEEDS A JOB. GRAB HER!"

She continued, "I used to do factory work like putting computer keyboards together," she continued.

What did he have to lose? He hadn't had any luck finding an aide anywhere else. The worst thing that would happen was she could think he was trying to pick her up and he'd get slapped. "How would you like to work for me?" He spelled out the words she didn't understand.

"What is the job?"

He pulled out one of his notes that explained the kind of help he needed and handed it to her.

She read the job description. "Don't you need someone like a nurse?" Margie asked.

"Not really. I just need help doing things."

Margie guessed at Jerry's words until she understood them or he spelled the words she couldn't get. Suddenly the place seemed to have a thousand people coming through the door. Then she said, "Let's go outside and talk. You probably don't want the whole world to know your business."

"You're right."

Jerry followed Margie out to her silver-colored pickup truck and she opened the driver's side and sat down. "This is better." Said Margie.

Jerry wheeled close to the truck door.

Looking at his note, she said, "I see you pay five-fifty an hour and I would work from eight a.m. to eleven a.m. and then I would come back at four p.m. to six p.m. to feed you dinner. So, the middle of the day would be free?"

"Yes."

"Don't you need help getting into bed?"

"I can do that myself. You turn back my bed before you leave at six."

"Remember, I haven't ever done this type of work before. My son is twenty, so it has been a long, long time since I have given him a bath."

"Margie, I think you will do just fine. Megan, my helper, will be around a few days to show you the ropes."

"Okay. When do I start?"

"Tomorrow morning at eight." He spelt out his address on his letter board and Margie wrote it down.

"See you in the morning."

Jerry was singing "I found a new aide" over and over all the way home.

Jerry was still humming when he arrived at his apartment. He transferred to his other wheelchair and went into his bedroom to call Megan. He glanced at the answering machine and noticed there was a message. Probably someone calling about the job. He would give the person Sam's phone number.

He reached across and pushed the button on the answering machine and listened to the message. "Hello Jerry, call me when you get a chance. There are some things we need to talk about." It was Betty. He excitedly reached for the stick he used to dial the phone.

He had been wanting to talk to her but hadn't known what to say. She might have been angry. After all, he had moved kind of fast asking her to marry him. Or, maybe something had happened and she needed help.

Jerry dialed Betty's number. Betty picked up the phone after only the second ring. "Hello."

"Hi, Betty."

"Jerry! It's so good to hear your voice."

"It's good to hear you too." He smiled.

"What have you been doing? You said you were going to call me."

"I know. I have been busy searching for someone to take Megan's place."

"Did you find someone?"

"Yes, her name is Margie. I think she is going to work out. And, Betty, I haven't called because I didn't know what to say after what happened."

"Jerry, can't we just continue seeing each other and not worry about the future right now?"

"That sounds great." He thought his heart was going to bounce out of his chest.

"What are you doing tomorrow night?" She asked him.

"Nothing."

"I could pick up some spaghetti and come over after work."

"I would like that very much."

"Jerry."

"Yes?"

"Would you like me to bring my kimono?"

"Yes, indeed."

"Good night, handsome." She hung up the phone.

Jerry dialed Megan's number.

"Hello?"

"You're a free woman." He laughed.

"What are you talking about?"

"Guess what you're doing in the morning, my fair lady?"

"I have to get this crazy old man out of bed."

"How would you like to train my new aide?"

"What? Did someone answer the ad? Did Sam find someone for you?"

"No. I went to Jack in the Box and met this woman named Margie. She was looking for a job and I hired her."

"This isn't one of your sick jokes? I was just trying to think of what we were going to do."

"No joke. I passed out all my notes and decided to stop for a Coke before coming home and that's where I met Margie."

"Do you think she will work out? Do you like her?"

"Yes, I think she will take good care of me. She seemed considerate and she didn't have much trouble understanding me."

"Jerry, that's great news. Wait a second." Jerry heard her go to the door and in a few seconds she came back. "Bob just came over with a pizza. He said that he was glad you found someone. I guess I'll see you in the morning to start training Margie."

"Yes. Enjoy your pizza. Oh, by the way, I spoke to Betty just now. Things are looking better."

"That's great. I'll see you tomorrow at eight."

"Megan."

"What?"

"I love you."

"I love you too, Jerry." She hung up the phone.

Epilogue - Joe's Life Now

At 70, Life is Good

Published in the Fresno Bee, Letters to the Editor, July 4, 2014

I am 70 years old and have had cerebral palsy since birth. For many years, I could be by myself for several hours during the day and then all night while I was sleeping. Now, I have people stay with me around the clock because I need help with getting in and out of bed.

This was a hard transition for me, but after surgery and a six-week stay in the hospital, I was weak and not able to be alone. I thought it would be temporary. I was wrong.

On the positive side of getting older, and perhaps giving up some independence, I am able to eat when I am hungry, go to the bathroom when I need to, have ice added to my water and coffee, and take a nap whenever I get tired. I also like being able to stay up late at night reading books and working on my writing.

Maybe it isn't so bad being older and needing more help. I don't know. My life is working. I am safe. I am comfortable, and I am still in control of my life. So, it is good.

Joe Hemphill

More Photographs

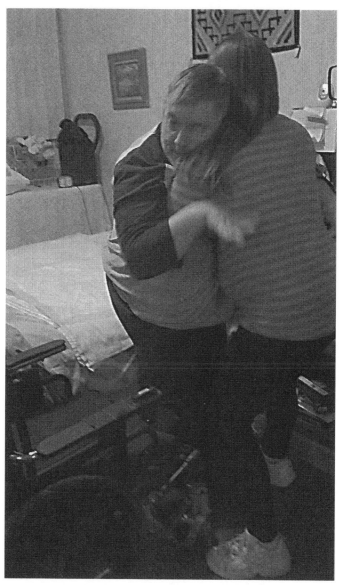

Needing more help getting out of bed.

Life is Good!

Claudia and Joe checking the time.

One of Joe's letters to the editor published in the local newspaper.

I hope you enjoyed this book.
This is me (Joe) at the beach in 2015.

Made in the USA
Middletown, DE
24 March 2019